SOLUTIONS TO INTERNATIONAL FINANCIAL REPORTING STANDARDS

3rd Edition

SOLUTIONS TO CASES IN INTERNATIONAL FINANCIAL REPORTING STANDARDS

3rd Edition

Derry Cotter, FCA

Published by
Chartered Accountants Ireland
Chartered Accountants House
47–49 Pearse Street
Dublin 2
www.charteredaccountants.ie

ISBN: 978-1-908199-44-7

First published 2008
Second edition 2009
Third edition 2012

Typeset by Compuscript
Printed by Turner's Printing

TABLE OF CONTENTS
(With Case Study Topics)

These solutions have been prepared as a resource to lecturers when using this book in a lecture or tutorial format. The solutions are numbered as per the case book and presented in the same order. The solutions in this text have been drafted in accordance with standards issued on or before 30 June 2012.

The following acronyms are used in journal entries throughout the book:

SOCI for the statement of comprehensive income

P/L for profit or loss

OCI for other comprehensive income

SOFP for the statement of financial position

Page

SOLUTION TO
BELLMOTH GROUP

(a) Goodman Hart and Company

Memo

To: **Yvonne Russell**

From: Bill Baxter

Date: 3 February 2x06

**Re: The Bellmoth Group Financial Statements for the year ended
31 December 2x05**

The following accounting issues have arisen as a result of the 2x05 audit:

(1) Caterpillar

(i) *Restructuring*
IAS 37 states that a provision for restructuring should only be recognised when the general recognition criteria for provisions are met. These criteria are outlined in paragraph 14 of IAS 37:

- An entity has a present obligation (legal or constructive) as a result of a past event;
- It is probable that an outflow of resources will be required to settle the obligation;
- A reliable estimate can be made of the amount of the obligation.

Additionally IAS 37 states that a constructive obligation to restructure arises only when an entity has;

- a detailed formal plan for the restructuring; and
- raised a valid expectation in those affected that it will carry out the restructuring by starting to implement that plan or announcing its main features to those affected by it (IAS 37.72).

These recognition criteria appear to have been satisfied in respect of Caterpillar's intention to downsize the provision of short-life foodstuffs. In identifying costs that can be recognised within a restructuring provision, IAS 37 states that … *a restructuring provision shall include only the direct expenditures arising from the restructuring, which are those that are both:*

- *necessarily entailed by the restructuring; and*
- *not associated with the ongoing activities of the entity* (IAS 37.80).

On the basis of the above requirements, the following amounts should be provided for by Caterpillar at 31 December 2x05:

	€'000
Loss on disposal of non-current assets	650
Redundancy settlements	350
	1,000

IAS 37 states that *provisions shall not be recognised for future operating losses* (para. 63).

IAS 37 also specifically excludes marketing costs from being included in a provision, on the basis that they:

- relate to the future conduct of the business and are not liabilities for restructuring at the end of the reporting period (IAS 37.81).

Warehouse re-design costs which will be incurred by Caterpillar are excluded on the same basis.

Thus, on the basis that Caterpillar is committed to the rationalisation of the short-life foodstuffs range, the following entry will be required in the 2x05 consolidated financial statements:

	DR €'000	CR €'000
Provision for loss on restructuring – SOCI P/L	1,000	
Provision for loss on restructuring – SOFP		1,000

(ii)   *Warranty provisions and refunds*

Warranty provisions are specifically addressed in Appendix C of IAS 37. It is concluded that it is appropriate that a provision should be made for the best estimate of the costs of making good, under the warranty, products sold before the end of the reporting period. Thus, a provision of €1.5 million should be set up in Caterpillar's 2x05 financial statements.

Similarly, although there is no legal compulsion for the company to make cash refunds, this has been the established practice, so as to promote customer loyalty. On the basis that it is probable that cash refunds of €800,000 will be made during 2x06, the gross margin recorded on these sales in 2x05 should be provided for.

The **exchange** of goods sold in 2x05 will merely result in a change in inventory records, and will have no effect on the company's recorded profit.

Thus, the following adjusting entries will be required in respect of the 2x05 consolidated financial statements:

	DR €'000	CR €'000
Warranty provision – SOCI P/L	1,500	
Warranty provision – SOFP		1,500
(Being provision for warranty on goods sold in 2x05)		
Provision for cash refunds – SOCI P/L	400	
Provision for cash refunds – SOFP		400
(Being provision for cash refunds)		

(iii)   Staff retraining costs

Legislative changes at European level resulting in more stringent product design will result in staff retraining costs over the next three years. IAS 37 (example 7 Appendix C), in respect of staff retraining, states that ... *there is no obligation because no obligating event (retraining) has taken place.*

Therefore no provision should be made at 31 December 2x05 in respect of the future retraining costs that will be incurred due to European legislative changes.

(iv)   Joint Venture

IFRS 11 *Joint Arrangements* defines a joint venture as a joint arrangement whereby the parties that have joint control of the arrangement have rights to the net assets of the arrangement (IFRS 11.16).

Caterpillar's investment in Bumble Bee appears to qualify as a joint venture as defined by IFRS 11.

IFRS 11 requires that a joint venturer shall recognise its interest in a joint venture using the equity method (IFRS 11.24).

Thus, the following adjusting entries are required in relation to the draft consolidated financial statements of the group for the year ended 31 December 2x05:

	DR €'000	CR €'000
Investment in Joint Venture	1,000	
Loan		1,000

The profits of Bumble Bee for the year ended 31 December 2x05 should be recorded in the consolidated financial statements as follows:

	DR €'000	CR €'000
Investment in Joint Venture	700	
Share of profit of joint venture – SOCI P/L		700

(being 50% of the after tax profit of Bumble Bee for the period ended 31 December 2x05).

The loan raised by Caterpillar to finance the acquisition of Bumble Bee is a financial liability. In accordance with IFRS 9, it should be accounted for, net of transaction costs, at fair value. Thus, the following journal is required:

	DR €'000	CR €'000
Bank	955	
Loan		955

1000–20–2 (handwritten)

Where a joint venturer sells assets to a joint venture, while the assets are retained by the joint venture, the joint venturer shall recognise only that portion of the gain or loss that is attributable to the interests of the other venturers (IAS 28.28).

As 50% of the goods sold by Caterpillar to Bumble Bee remain in the inventory of the joint venture at the year end, the following consolidation adjustment is required:

	DR €'000	CR €'000
Cost of sales	75	
Investment in Joint Venture		75

(being elimination of Caterpillar's share of unrealised inter-company profit on inventory,

i.e. Inter-company sales × profit margin × % held in inventory × Caterpillar's shareholding in Bumble Bee

i.e. (€1 million × 30% × 50% × 50%).

(handwritten margin notes:)
good of 1 million
half remain in stock
= 500
× 30%
= 150 × 5
= 75
JV sh

Bumble Bee's operating results are included in the consolidated financial statements of the Bellmoth Group on an equity basis. Thus, as the inventory of Bumble Bee is *not* included in the financial statements of the Group, there is no adjustment to inventory in the above journal entry.

Disclosure issues:

It will also be necessary to consider the disclosure requirements of IAS 24 *Related Party Disclosures.* As joint venturer and joint venture, Caterpillar and Bumble Bee are classified as related parties by the standard, thus requiring the following disclosures in the financial statements of Caterpillar, Bumble Bee and in the consolidated financial statements:

- Description of the relationship between them (joint venturer and joint venture);
- The amounts involved (Sales of €1 million in the year ended 31 December 2x05);
- Any other elements of the transaction necessary for an understanding of its effect on the financial statements;
- The amounts due to or from the related parties, and provisions for doubtful debts due from such parties (IAS 24.18).

(v)   *Tangible non-current assets*

(I)   Sale of land
Land which was sold during 2x05 for €1.3 million continues to be included in the draft financial statements at 31 December 2x05. The following amending entries will therefore be required, in accordance with IAS 16 *Property, Plant and Equipment,* to record the disposal:

	DR €'000	CR €'000
Bank	1,300	
Land		800
Profit on disposal – SOCI P/L*		500
Revaluation surplus – SOFP	200	
Retained earnings – SOFP		200

*In accordance with IAS 1, subject to materiality, the profit on disposal should be separately disclosed in the statement of comprehensive income or in the notes (IAS 1.97).

(II)   Investment property
IAS 40 *Investment Property* requires that an entity shall choose as its accounting policy either the fair value model or the cost model for all of its investment property (IAS 40.30). Caterpillar has opted for the fair value model, and IAS 40 requires in this instance that changes in value be recorded in profit or loss for the period.

There has been an impairment of the investment property during 2x05, resulting from a rezoning decision. The following amending entry will therefore be required to the 2x05 draft financial statements:

	DR €'000	CR €'000
Impairment write-down – SOCI P/L	400	
Investment property		400

(Being impairment of investment property)

(2) Butterfly

(i) *Inventory*

The use of uniform accounting policies within a group is required by IFRS 10 *Consolidated Financial Statements* (IFRS 10.19). It should also be noted that IAS 2 *Inventories* requires that the costs for most inventories be assigned by using either FIFO or the weighted average cost formula (IAS 2.25).

It will therefore be necessary to change the LIFO valuation basis used by Butterfly for its wool inventories, so as to bring this into line with the FIFO basis used in the rest of the Bellmoth group.

	$'000
LIFO basis:	
8 tons at $50,000 per ton	400
7 tons at $60,000 per ton	420
2 tons at $70,000 per ton	140
	960
FIFO basis:	
9 tons at $70,000 per ton	630
8 tons at $60,000 per ton	480
	1,110

It will be necessary therefore to increase the value of raw material inventory by $150,000. This equates to an increase of €100,000 when translated into €s. Therefore, the following adjusting journal entry is required to the draft 2x05 consolidated financial statements:

	DR €'000	CR €'000
Inventory – SOFP	100	
Cost of sales		100*

In accordance with IAS 2 *Inventories,* it is not necessary to reduce raw material inventory to its net realisable value, as long as the finished products into which it will be incorporated are expected to be sold at or above cost (IAS 2.32). It is assumed that this is the case in respect of Butterfly's inventory of wool.

*At the end of the Consolidated SOCI, profit for the year is divided between the owners of the parent and NCI. Non-controlling interests' share of Butterfly's profit will be increased by €20,000 at that point.

SOLUTION TO
CROMPTON PLANT AND
FERTILISER GROUP

Memorandum

To: **Ms J. Smith, Finance Director**

From: **Ralph Thornton**

Date: **20 July 2x06**

Subject: (1) Accounting issues relating to Plant Life Limited
(2) Accounting issues relating to other companies in the Group
(3) Supplementary information

(1) Accounting issues relating to Plant Life Limited

(a) *Cost of acquisition of Plant Life Limited*
IFRS 3 requires that the consideration transferred in a business combination shall be measured at fair value, which shall be calculated as the sum of:

- the acquisition date fair value of assets transferred by the acquirer,
- liabilities incurred, and
- equity interests issued by the acquirer (IFRS 3.37).

(i) Equity Shares issued
The 1 million shares issued by Crompton Holdings Limited should be recorded at fair value as follows (IFRS 3.37):

	DR €'000	CR €'000
Investment in Plant Life Limited	6,000	
Ordinary share capital		1,000
Share premium		5,000

(ii)   **Financial asset**

The investment in Grafton Bank plc shares is a financial asset and it should be regarded as being disposed of for a realised value of €1.35 million. IFRS 3 requires that any resulting gain or loss should be recognised by Crompton Holdings Limited in profit or loss as follows (IFRS 3.38):

	DR €'000	CR €'000
Investment in Plant Life Limited	1,350	
Financial asset		1,000
Profit on disposal of financial asset – SOCI P/L		350

Separate disclosure in the SOCI, or in the notes, should be considered, in accordance with IAS 1, subject to materiality (IAS 1.97).

(iii)   **Deferred cash consideration**

The acquisition of Plant Life Limited also involves deferred cash consideration of €400,000 which is contingent on certain profitability targets being achieved.

IFRS 3 requires that an acquirer shall recognise the acquisition-date fair value of contingent consideration as part of the consideration transferred in exchange for the acquiree (IFRS 3.39). At the acquisition date, the fair value of the contingent consideration appeared to be zero, as the directors of Crompton Holdings Limited were confident that Plant Life would not achieve the necessary profitability targets.

IFRS 3 also states that *changes* in the fair value of contingent consideration resulting from events such as meeting profitability targets, are **not** measurement period adjustments, and must therefore be recognised in accordance with IFRS 9, IAS 37 or other IFRSs as appropriate (IFRS 3.58).

Payment of the cash consideration of €400,000 became probable on the 1 July 2x06 (before the financial statements were authorised for issue), as the awarding of a new contract to Plant Life meant that the required profitability targets were likely to be achieved.

This change constitutes an adjusting event after the reporting period, as defined by IAS 10, and a provision for payment of the cash consideration should be recognised in the financial statements for the year ended 31 May 2x06.

IAS 37 states that, when the effect of the time value of money is material, the amount of a provision shall be the present value of the expenditure expected to be required to settle the obligation (IAS 37.45).

Therefore, the following journal entry is required in respect of the deferred cash consideration:

	DR €'000	CR €'000
Acquisition costs – SOCI P/L	330	
Non-current liabilities		330

(Being fair value of deferred consideration of €400,000 discounted for 2 years @ 10% p.a.)

(iv) Acquisition expenses

The acquirer shall account for acquisition-related costs as expenses in the periods in which the costs are incurred (IFRS 3.53). The professional fees and general management expenses should therefore be charged to the profit or loss of Crompton Holdings Limited in the year ended 31 May 2x06.

	DR €'000	CR €'000
Acquisition costs – SOCI P/L	185	
Trade and other payables		100
Trade and other receivables		85

(b) *Allocation of the cost of the business combination to the assets and liabilities assumed*

(i) Inventories

The finished goods inventory of Plant Life Limited is included in its financial statements at €1.469 million, on a FIFO basis, at 31 May 2x06. However IFRS 3 states that an acquirer shall recognise an acquiree's identifiable assets at their acquisition date fair values (IFRS 3.18).

Fair value is defined as:

'...the price that would be received to sell an asset in an orderly transaction between market participants (IFRS 13, Appendix A).

As the inventory of Plant Life Limited was sold for €200,000 less than its book value, the following adjusting journal entry is required:

	DR €'000	CR €'000
Retained earnings of Plant Life @ acquisition date	200	
Inventory		200

(ii) Reorganisation programme

IFRS 3 states that the acquirer shall recognise only the consideration transferred for the acquiree and the assets acquired and liabilities assumed in the exchange for the acquiree. Separate transactions should be accounted for in accordance with the relevant IFRSs (IFRS 3.51).

The fact that the Board of Directors of Plant Life Limited was already committed to the reorganisation programme prior to its acquisition by the Crompton Group, means that the costs of the programme should be regarded as a liability assumed at the acquisition date.

IFRS 3 also states that the acquirer shall measure an acquired non-current asset that is classified as held for sale at the acquisition date, at fair value less costs to sell, in accordance with IFRS 5 (IFRS 3.31). Thus, it will be necessary to write the value of machinery down by an amount of €100,000.

	DR	**CR**
	€'000	€'000
Retained earnings of Plant Life @ acquisition date	350	
Machinery Write down		100
Trade and other payables Provision		250

(Being write-down of machine and liability for re-organisation costs at acquisition date)

The machinery should also be separately classified in the statement of financial position as 'assets held for sale' in accordance with IFRS 5, thus necessitating the following journal entry: [IFRS 5]

	DR	**CR**
	€'000	€'000
Assets held for sale	300	
Machinery		300

(Being machinery re-classified at fair value less costs to sell)

(iii) Legal action

IFRS 3 states that, if the initial accounting for a business combination is incomplete by the end of the reporting period, the acquirer shall report provisional amounts for the items for which the accounting is incomplete (IFRS 3.45). IFRS 3 also requires that the acquirer should, during the measurement period, retrospectively adjust the provisional amounts to reflect new information obtained about facts and circumstances that existed at the acquisition date. The measurement period shall not exceed one year from the acquisition date (IFRS 3.45).

In the case of Plant Life Limited, a gain of €320,000 was realised on 20 June 2x06, prior to the date on which the financial statements of the group were authorised for issue. This is an adjusting event after the reporting period, as defined by IAS 10, and it should replace the gain of €100,000 estimated at 31 May 2x06. The financial statements of Plant Life Limited should be adjusted as follows:

	DR €'000	CR €'000
Trade and other receivables	220	
Retained earnings of Plant Life @ acquisition date		220

(iv) Land and buildings

The land and buildings of Plant Life Limited should be restated to their fair value at 31 May 2x06 (IFRS 3.18). The following adjustment will be required:

	DR €'000	CR €'000
Land and buildings	202	
Revaluation surplus at acquisition date		202

IFRS 3 also requires that an acquirer should recognise and measure a deferred tax liability, arising from an asset acquired in a business combination, in accordance with IAS 12 *Income Taxes* (IFRS 3.24).

This will give rise to a temporary difference, as outlined in IAS 12, which will affect goodwill arising on acquisition (IAS 12.19). As the capital gains tax rate is 20%, this will necessitate the following journal entry:

	DR €'000	CR €'000
Revaluation surplus @ acquisition date	40.4	
Provision for deferred tax – SOFP		40.4

(v) Dividend

In July 2x06, Plant Life Limited paid a dividend of €600,000 out of its profits of the year ended 31 May 2x06. IAS 27, *Separate Financial Statements*, requires that an entity should recognise a dividend from a subsidiary in profit or loss in its separate financial statements when its right to receive the dividend is established (IAS 27.12). Likewise, IAS 10, *Events after the Reporting Period*, states that, if an entity declares a dividend after the reporting period, the dividend should not be recognised as a liability at the end of the reporting period (IAS 10.12).

Thus, the dividend will be recorded by Plant Life and Crompton Holdings as follows in the year ending 31 May 2x07:

	DR €'000	CR €'000
Retained earnings (SOFP)	600	
Bank		600

(Being payment of dividend by Plant Life)

Bank	600	
Dividend received – SOCI P/L		600

(Being receipt of dividend by Crompton Holdings Limited)

(2) Accounting issues relating to other companies in the Group

(i)   Leisure centre

The leisure centre is *not* an asset of the group at 31 May 2x06. In substance the rights to future economic benefits will accrue almost exclusively to the employees' pension fund. The investment property should therefore be removed from Ingston's Statement of Financial Position at 31 May 2x06.

Ingston, however, does have a different asset in the form of the five years' rental income from the leisure centre. On the assumption that the ultimate cash realisation can be assessed with reasonable certainty, the flow of rental inflows should be recognised in Ingston Limited's financial statements at 31 May 2x06, at their fair value. In order to determine the fair value, it will be necessary to discount the rental inflows to present value, at the Group's cost of borrowed funds of 10%. Using annuity tables, the present value of the rental inflows is €454,920 (€120,000 × 3.791).

The following adjustments will be required to the financial statements of the Group at 31 May 2x06:

	DR €'000	CR €'000
Revaluation of investment property – SOCI P/L	1,000*	
Provision for pension fund deficiency – SOFP	3,000**	
Investment property		4,000

*Being reversal of previous upward revaluation of investment property through profit or loss

**Being re-classification of cost of investment property, as being offset against pension fund deficiency

	DR €'000	CR €'000
Trade and other receivables	455	
Deferred income – SOFP		455

(Being recognition of future rental inflows from leisure centre)

Workings

Summary of journal adjustments

(a) *Accounting issues relating to Plant Life Limited for year ended 31 May 2x06*

	DR €'000	CR €'000
Investment in Plant Life Limited	6,000	
Ordinary share capital		1,000
Share premium		5,000
(Being acquisition of Plant Life in books of Crompton Holdings)		
Investment in Plant Life Limited	1,350	
Financial asset		1,000
Profit on disposal of financial asset – SOCI P/L		350
(Being acquisition of Plant Life in books of Crompton Holdings)		

Acquisition costs – SOCI P/L	330	
Non-current liabilities		330

(Being fair value of deferred
  consideration paid by Crompton
  Holdings)

Retained earnings of Plant Life at acquisition date	200	
Inventory		200

(Being correction of overstatement of
  Plant Life Ltd's inventory at acquisition
  date)

Acquisition costs – SOCI P/L	100	
Trade and other payables		100

(Being professional fees due in
  respect of acquisition of Plant Life)

Operating expenses – SOCI P/L	85	
Trade and other receivables		85

(Being general expenses incurred
  which are charged to expense)

Retained earnings of Plant Life at acquisition date	350	
Machinery		100
Trade and other payables		250

(Being restructuring provision at
  acquisition date)

Assets held for sale	300	
Machinery		300

(Being re-classification of machinery
  as a non-current asset held for sale)

Trade and other receivables	220	
Retained earnings of Plant Life @ acquisition		220

(Being debtor in respect of legal
action by Plant Life)

Land and buildings	202	
Revaluation surplus @ acquisition		202
(Being re-statement of land &		
buildings to fair value at date		
of acquisition)		

Revaluation surplus @ acquisition	40.4	
Provision for deferred tax – SOFP		40.4
(Being deferred tax on revaluation		
surplus)		

(b) *Accounting issues relating to other companies in the Group:*

Reversal of investment property		
revaluation – SOCI P/L	1,000	
Provision for pension fund		
deficiency – SOFP	3,000	
Investment property		4,000
(Being re-classification of leisure centre)		

Trade and other receivables	455	
Deferred income – SOFP		455
(Being rentals receivable from leisure centre)		

(c) *Calculation of goodwill arising on the acquisition of Plant Life Limited*

Cost of control account in Plant Life Limited

	€'000		€'000
Investment in Plant Life Ltd	6,000	Ordinary share cap.	100
Investment in Plant Life Ltd	1,350	Share premium	250
Retained earnings (inventory)	200	Revaluation surplus	1,000
Retained earnings (reorg. costs)	350	Retained earnings	4,927
Revaluation surplus (def. tax)	40	Ret earnings (legal action)	220
		Revaluation Surplus	202
		Goodwill*	1,241
	7,940		7,940

* Goodwill is computed as follows in accordance with IFRS 3 *Business Combinations (IFRS 3.32):*

Alternative presentation:

	€
Consideration transferred at fair value (€6m + €1.35m)	7,350,000
Less, fair value of the acquisition-date amounts of the identifiable assets acquired and the liabilities assumed (€6.277m − €200k − €350k + €220k + €202k − €40.4k)	(6,108,600)
Goodwill	1,241,400

SOLUTION TO
CURRENT ISSUES GROUP

Report

Subject: Accounting issues relating to the financial statements for the year ended 31 December 2x05

Prepared for: A. Dorgan, Finance Director

Prepared by: X. Erox

Date: 1 March 2x06

Contents

1. **Summary of group structure**

2. **Accounting treatment**

   (a) Investments

   (b) Related party issues

   (c) Sale of assets

   (d) Financing

   (e) Titles

   (f) Impairment of assets

   (g) Miscellaneous impairment issues

   (h) Miscellaneous provisions and contingency issues

(1) Group structure

As at 31 December 2x05, Current Issues Limited had the following subsidiary undertakings:

- Big Times Limited
- Blow the Whistle Limited
- Worthit Limited

At the same date Current Issues Limited also had an Associate, Sometimes Limited.

(2) Accounting treatment – Current Issues Group

(a)   Investments

(i)   Acquisition of Big Times Limited

	Parent	NCI
	€	
Consideration	800,000	
Non-controlling interests		120,000
Less fair value of identifiable		
net assets acquired	(400,000)	(100,000)
Goodwill	400,000	20,000

In accordance with IFRS 3 *Business Combinations,* goodwill should be recognised as an asset at the date of acquisition (IFRS 3.32).

(ii)   Investment in Sometimes Limited
Current Issues has significant influence in Sometimes Limited, by virtue of its 25% shareholding. Sometimes is therefore an associate of Current Issues (IAS 28.3).

(iii)   Acquisition of Blow the Whistle Limited
Blow the Whistle Limited is a subsidiary of Current Issues following the acquisition of a 75% shareholding in that company. Intra-group sales which have taken place during the year of

acquisition may have related party disclosure implications under IAS 24 *Related Party Disclosures*:

- Intra-group sales need not be disclosed in the *group financial statements,* as they will be cancelled on consolidation. The amount of sales that will be cancelled will be those that were made after acquisition (i.e. €600,000 × 70%)
- Disclosure of sales by Current Issues to Blow the Whistle after the 31 March 2x05 will be required in the separate financial statements of Current Issues and the individual financial statements of Blow the Whistle, as they are related parties from that date.

(iv) Acquisition of Worthit Limited

Worthit Limited is a subsidiary of Current Issues, following the acquisition of 80% of the equity shares in that company. The acquisition is regarded as a **bargain purchase** as the aggregate of the consideration transferred plus the amount of non-controlling interests is less than the fair value of identifiable net assets acquired:

	€'000
Consideration transferred	450
Non-controlling interests* (€700,000 × 20%)	140
	590
Fair value of identifiable net assets acquired	(700)
	110

* IFRS 3 states that an acquirer shall measure any non-controlling interest in an acquiree either at fair value or at the non-controlling interest's share of the acquiree's identifiable net assets (IFRS 3.19). The latter method of measurement is adopted for this acquisition.

IFRS 3 states that an acquirer should recognise the resulting gain in profit or loss on the acquisition date (IFRS 3.34). However, before doing so, the acquirer should reassess whether it has correctly identified all of the assets acquired and all of the liabilities assumed. The acquirer is then required to review the measurement procedures used (IFRS 3.36). On the assumption that Current Issues has satisfied these requirements, the following journal entry is required in the consolidated financial statements:

	DR	CR
	€'000	€'000
Net assets	110	
Gain on bargain purchase – SOCI P/L		110

(b) *Related party issues*

(i) Loan

Mr Smith, being a director of Current Issues, is regarded as part of the company's key management personnel by IAS 24 *Related Party Disclosures*, and is therefore identified as a related party by the standard (IAS 24.9(d)). Subject to materiality, details relating to the loan to Mr Smith should be disclosed in the financial statements of Current Issues, and of the Group. The following disclosures will be required:

- Description of the relationship between the related parties (Director of Current Issues);
- The amounts involved (Loan of €1 million);
- Any other elements of the transaction necessary for an understanding of the financial statements;
- The amounts due to or from the related parties at the end of the reporting period, and provisions for doubtful debts due from such parties at that date (IAS 24.18).

(ii) Sale of printing press

- *Sale of printing press by Current Issues to Big Times*
  As Big Times and Current Issues are subsidiary and parent respectively, they are defined as related parties (IAS 24.9(b)). Subject to its materiality, details of this sale should therefore be disclosed in the individual/separate financial statements of both companies.

  As the inter-company sale will be cancelled on consolidation, disclosure in the group financial statements is not required.

- *Gift of printing press by Sometimes to Big Times*
  Sometimes and Big Times are related parties. This transaction will therefore need to be disclosed as follows, subject to its materiality:
  - the individual financial statement of Big Times;

- the individual financial statements of Sometimes; and
- the consolidated financial statements of the Current Issues Group.

(iii) Purchase of dye by Sometimes from Fine Tune
Neither Sometimes nor Fine Tune is a member of the Current Issues group. Therefore, no disclosure issues arise which are relevant to the group.

As Sometimes and Fine Tune are subject to common control, they are deemed to be related parties (IAS 24.9(a)). Therefore, details of the purchase of dye should be disclosed in the financial statements of both companies.

(c) *Sale of assets*

(i) Sale of freehold land by Current Issues to Money Limited
The IASB Conceptual Framework requires that financial statements should reflect the substance of transactions, and not necessarily their legal form (Chapter 4.6). In substance, the monies received by Current Issues from Money Limited represent a loan arrangement rather than a sale. This is so because Current Issues continues to incur the risks of ownership of the asset, and to derive the potential benefits therefrom. The put and call options which are in place have the effect of ensuring that the land will again become the legal property of Current Issues after two years have elapsed.

The following entry should be made to record the amounts received from Money Limited:

	DR €'000	CR €'000
Bank	700	
Loan		700

(ii) Purchase and sale of freehold buildings by Current Issues
The accounting treatment employed in respect of these buildings since the date of purchase should be as follows:

	DR €'000	CR €'000
Freehold buildings	300	
Bank		300
(Being purchase of asset 1 Jan 2x02)		
Depreciation expense	6	
Accumulated depreciation		6
(Being depr. charge for 2x02)		
Depreciation expense	6	
Accumulated depreciation		6
(Being depr. charge for 2x03)		
Accumulated depreciation	12	
Freehold buildings		12
(Being cancellation of accumulated depreciation)		
Freehold buildings	212	
Revaluation surplus – SOCI OCI		212
(Being reval. of bldg at 31 Dec. 2x03 – deferred tax is ignored as per instruction in question)		
Depreciation expense	10.4	
Accumulated depreciation		10.4
(Being depr. charge for 2x04: €500k/48)		
Revaluation surplus – SOFP	4.4	
Retained earnings – SOFP		4.4
(Being amortisation of revaluation surplus to retained earnings for 2x04: i.e. €212,000/48)*		
Bank	600	
Accumulated depr.	10.4	
Profit on disposal – SOCI P/L		110.4**
Freehold buildings		500
(Being disposal of bldg in 2x05)		

Revaluation surplus – SOFP   207.6

Retained earnings – SOFP   207.6

(Being transfer of balance on
Revaluation surplus to Retained
Earnings on disposal in 2x05)

*This annual transfer is optional, in accordance with IAS 16.41.

**Subject to materiality considerations, separate disclosure may be required in the Statement of Comprehensive Income or in the notes (IAS 1.97).

(d)   *Financing*

(i)   Incorporation of Fudgeit Limited

Although the setting up of Fudgeit Limited has the form of a joint arrangement, there is a lack of joint control, which is a required component of a joint arrangement (IFRS 11.4). Thus, it appears in substance to be an attempt to exclude a loan of €500,000 from the group financial statements of Current Issues. Under the equity method, the loan obtained by Fudgeit is totally excluded from the statement of financial position of the Group.

IFRS 10 *Consolidated Financial Statements* states that an investor controls an investee when the investor is exposed or has rights, to variable returns … and has the ability to affect those returns through its power over the investee (IFRS 10.7). Through its control of the Board of Directors of Fudgeit, Current Issues has the ability to affect its variable returns from its investment in that company.

Fudgeit should therefore be regarded as a subsidiary of Current Issues and its financial statements should be consolidated as part of the group.

(ii)   Arrangement with Advance Factors

The agreement with Advance Factors is primarily a non-recourse factoring agreement, with Current Issues only being liable for the first €10,000 of bad debts. The normal level of bad debts incurred by Current Issues is 3% of gross debtors, which at the time of the factoring agreement amounted to

€1 million. Therefore, the risks and rewards of ownership relating to the debtors appear to have substantially passed to Advance Factors.

The following amounts should therefore be included in the group statement of financial position in relation to the debtors factored by Current Issues:

	€'000
Current Assets	
Trade receivables	250
Current Liabilities	
Trade and other payables	59.5*

*Trade and other payables include the following:	
Accrued interest & fees	€49,500
Provision for Factor's recourse to Current Issues	€10,000
	€59,500

(e)   Titles

(i)   Internally generated titles

IAS 38 states that *Internally generated brands, mastheads, publishing titles, customer lists and items similar in substance shall not be recognised as intangible assets* (IAS 38.63).

Thus, the sums expended by Current Issues in promoting the Group's titles should not be capitalised, but should be expensed to profit or loss as they are incurred.

The fact that expenditure of €450,000 on internal titles was included as an asset in the statement of financial position of Current Issues at 31 December 2x04, constitutes a prior period error. Should this error be deemed material, IAS 8 requires a retrospective restatement of items affected in an entity's financial statements:

- Restating the comparative amounts for the prior period(s) presented in which the error occurred; *or*

- If the error occurred before the earliest prior period presented, restating the opening balances of assets, liabilities, and equity for the earliest prior period presented (IAS 8.42).

In the case of retrospective restatement, IAS 1, *Presentation of Financial Statements,* also requires that a statement of financial position be presented at the beginning of the earliest comparative period (IAS 1.10 (f)).

The following journal entry will reflect the net effect of correcting the error in the financial statements of Current Issues and those of the Group:

	DR €'000	CR €'000
Retained earnings	450	
Intangible assets		450

(ii) Titles purchased from No Time Limited

These titles represent an intangible asset obtained by means of separate acquisition. Such assets are always considered to give rise to probable future economic benefits that will accrue to an entity (IAS 38.25). As the cost can also be reliably measured, the titles purchased from No Time Limited fully satisfy the criteria to be recognised as an asset (IAS 38.21).

These titles, like all intangible assets, should be measured initially at cost (IAS 38.24). Subsequently, an entity is required to choose either the cost model or the revaluation model as its accounting policy. If the revaluation model is chosen, all other assets in the same class should be accounted for similarly, unless there is no active market for those assets (IAS 38.72). It is not usually appropriate to revalue intangible assets, as there is rarely an active market for such assets.

Current Issues appears to have adopted the cost model for the titles acquired from No Time Limited. Thus, the titles should be carried at their cost of €100,000, less any accumulated amortisation and any accumulated impairment losses (IAS 38.74).

(f)   *Impairment of assets*

IAS 36, *Impairment of Assets,* requires an impairment review to be carried out where indicators of impairment suggest that a company's assets may not be fully recoverable (IAS 36.9). For this purpose, the 'e-learning division' is identified as a 'cash generating unit', and the impairment review process requires the following procedures to be employed:

- As the fair value less costs to sell (€500,000) of the assets of the division are less than the assets' net book value in the statement of financial position (€1.2m), a value in use computation is required.

- **Value in use computation:**

Terminal value of net assets of division (based on pre-tax and pre-finance costs as required by IAS 36.50)	€1.43 million*
Discount factor for year 5 using a discount rate of 16%	.4761
Present value of cash flows of cash generating unit	€680,000

*IAS 36 does not permit the inclusion of estimated future cash flows that are expected to arise from improving or enhancing an asset's performance. Thus, cash inflows of €1,400,000 resulting from planned development expenditure are not included (IAS 36.44). Software development costs are excluded on a similar basis.

The recoverable amount of the net assets of the 'e-learning division' is the *higher* of:

- Fair value less costs to sell of €500,000; and
- Value in use €680,000.

Thus, the recoverable amount is €680,000. As this is less than the value of the net assets (€1,200,000) in the statement of financial position, the value of the assets of the division should be reduced. The required reduction of €520,000 should be accounted for as follows, in accordance with IAS 36.104:

(i) Goodwill of €300,000 should be eliminated;
(ii) The balance of €220,000 should be written off against the other assets of the division, pro-rata on the basis of the carrying amount of each asset.

Therefore, the following journal entry is required:

	DR €'000	CR €'000
Impairment write-off – SOCI P/L	520	
Goodwill		300
Intangible non-current assets (€220k × (400k/900k))		98
Tangible non-current assets (€220k × (500k/900k))		122

These write-downs should be included in profit or loss for the year ended 31 December 2x05, and if material they should be separately disclosed in accordance with IAS 1.97.

(g) Miscellaneous impairment issues

(i) Printing Presses

As the reasons for the impairment write-downs of 2x03 have now been reversed, the printing presses should be restored to their recoverable amount (IAS 36.114). The extent to which depreciation has been reduced, due to the previous impairment write-down, must however be taken into account at the time of the reversal (IAS 36.117).

The amount of the impairment reversal must therefore be calculated as follows:

	€	€
Original impairment write-down (€200k – €60,000)		140,000

Depreciation in 2x04 if based on original cost (€400k/10)	40,000	
Actual depreciation in 2x04 (€60k/5)	(12,000)	
Under-depr. in 2x04 due to impairment write-down in 20x3		(28,000)
Impairment reversal in 2x05 (restricted)		112,000

This will restore the printing press to €160,000 (i.e. €112k + (€60k − €12k)) at 31 December 2x04, which is equivalent to what its NBV would have been (i.e. €400k × 40%) had the original impairment not been recorded.

The following journal entry is required to effect this adjustment:

	DR €	CR €
Tangible non-current assets	112,000	
Impairment write-back – SOCI P/L		112,000

(Being write back in 2x05 of previous impairment reversal)

The above write-back should be included in profit or loss in 2x05, and disclosed separately if material. The revised book value of €160,000 should be written off at 25% per annum on a straight line basis, commencing in 2x05.

(ii) Land

The revision of consumer preferences in 2x05 has meant that the amount at which the land was valued in 2x02 should now be reinstated as a conservative estimate of the asset's current value.

The following journal entry will be required to effect the reversal:

	DR €	CR €
Land	300,000	
Impairment write-back – SOCI P/L		100,000*
Revaluation surplus – SOCI OCI		200,000**

*Disclose separately if material.

**Deferred tax is ignored, as per instruction in question.

(iii) Titles

IAS 36 *Impairment of Assets* requires that an impairment loss recognised in prior periods (for an asset other than goodwill) shall be reversed if, and only if, there has been a change in the estimates used to determine the asset's recoverable amount since the last impairment loss was recognised (IAS 36.114). Clearly, improved content, which has led to the revision of consumer preferences, falls into this category. Therefore, the previous impairment loss should be reversed as follows:

	DR €	CR €
Intangible assets	250,000	
Reversal of impairment loss – SOCI P/L		250,000*

*Disclose separately if material.

(h)   Miscellaneous provisions and contingency issues

(i) Legal action

In accordance with IAS 37 *Provisions, Contingent Liabilities and Contingent Assets:*

In respect of the action taken by the celebrity plaintiff in November 2x05, it was clear on 31 December 2x05 that Current Issues had a present obligation resulting from a past event. On this basis, a provision should be recognised (IAS 37.14).

On 31 March 2x06, the date on which the financial statements are authorised for issue, legal opinion was that the plaintiff was likely to be awarded €100,000. This provides further evidence relating to a condition existing at the end of the reporting period, and it therefore constitutes an adjusting event after the reporting period date (IAS 10.3).

Therefore, a provision of €100,000 should be recognised at 31 December 2x05 in relation to the action being taken by the celebrity plaintiff. Provision should also be made for whatever legal costs may ensue if the action goes to court.

	DR €'000	CR €'000
Provision for legal claim – SOCI P/L	100	
Provision for legal claim – SOFP		100

- A contingent liability of €100,000 should be disclosed by way of note in the financial statements, in respect of the additional amount which might be awarded by the court (IAS 37.28). There is a risk of a transfer of economic benefits which, at a 25% level of probability, must be considered as being more than remote.

- The counter-claim made against a publicity group is a contingent asset (IAS 37.10). It is possible (but not virtually certain) that a cash settlement of €20,000 may be agreed. As an inflow of economic benefits is probable, details of the counter-claim should be disclosed by way of note in the financial statements (IAS 37.34).

(ii)   Review of provisions

- Restructuring costs should only be recognised as a provision when an entity has an *obligation* to carry out the restructuring (IAS 37.71). The preparation of a detailed formal plan which has begun to be implemented, or at least which has been discussed with parties likely to be affected, is evidence of such an obligation (IAS 37.72).

  As yet, only an outline plan for the restructuring has been prepared by Current Issues, and there is little evidence that the company is committed to proceeding with it. The provision of €250,000 should therefore be reversed as follows:

	DR €'000	CR €'000
Provision – SOFP	250	
Decrease in provision – SOCI P/L		250

This represents the correction of an error in the previous year. The adjustment is made in the 2x05 financial statements. If the error is deemed to be material, however, it would have to be corrected retrospectively in accordance with IAS 8 *Accounting Policies, Changes in Accounting Estimates and Errors.*

- Ongoing repairs should be charged to expense as they are incurred (IAS 16.12). The fact that a provision of €300,000 was set up by Current Issues for the ongoing repair of printing presses constitutes an error. If the error is considered material, the provision should be eliminated as follows in accordance with IAS 8.41:

  - €50,000 to be added back to profit for the year ended 31 December 2x05
  - €250,000 to be reversed retrospectively.

  Should the error **not** be deemed material, it should be reversed in its entirety in the 2x05 financial statements.
      The fact that a significant proportion of the provision will be required during 2x06 suggests that there may be grounds for carrying out an impairment review of the printing presses, as required by IAS 36 *Impairment of Assets.*

- IAS 16, *Property, Plant and Equipment,* requires that the initial estimate of the costs of dismantling and removing an asset be included in the asset's cost (IAS 16.16). On the basis that there is a present obligation to decommission the printing presses, resulting from a past event (i.e. their purchase), a decommissioning liability should be recognised, in accordance with IAS 37 *Provisions, Contingent Liabilities and Contingent Assets.*

  The estimated decommissioning expenses of €300,000 will therefore be recorded as follows:

	DR €'000	CR €'000
Plant & equipment	300	
Provision for decommissioning costs – SOFP		300

This will result in an increase in the depreciation charge in respect of plant and equipment.

(iii)   Payments to retired employees

The commitment to pay pensions to retired employees is an example of an onerous contract, as defined in IAS 37 *Provisions, Contingent Liabilities and Contingent Assets* (IAS 37.10). A contract is onerous when the unavoidable costs of meeting the obligations under it exceed the economic benefits expected to be received under it.

Thus, a provision should be made for the obligation to make the pension payments to the retired employees. The standard also requires that provisions should be discounted where the effect of doing so is material (IAS 37.45). The company's pre-tax WACC is considered an appropriate discount rate for this purpose (IAS 37.47):

	€	Disc. factor @ 12%*	PV
2x06	150,000	.893	133,950
2x07	200,000	.797	159,400
2x08	250,000	.712	178,000
2x09	280,000	.636	178,080
2x10	320,000	.567	181,440
2x11	350,000	.507	177,450
	1,550,000		1,008,320

*It is assumed that the obligation to make pension payments will arise on the last day of each year.

A provision of €1.008 million should be recognised in the financial statements at 31 December 2x05. If material, it will be disclosed separately in the Statement of Comprehensive Income or the notes, in accordance with IAS 1.

The following journal entry will be required:

	DR €'m	CR €'m
Provision for pension costs – SOCI P/L	1.008	
Provision for pension costs – SOFP		1.008

(i) Tangible Non-Current Assets

(i) Capitalisation of costs

The following should be capitalised as part of the construction cost of the mini-printing press, in accordance with IAS 16 *Property, Plant and Equipment*:

	€
• Machine part components (net of trade discount)	19,000
• Option premium (the construction of the printing press was probable when this cost was incurred)	3,000
• External labour costs	10,000
• Labour costs of own employees	13,000
• Safety procedure costs	2,000
• Trial print runs	2,000
• Financing costs	3,000
• Estimated dismantling costs	1,500
Total costs capitalised	53,500

Lecture note:

– The cost of correcting *design errors* is not capitalised as this is considered an 'abnormal cost' by IAS 16.22

– *Marketing costs* are not capitalised as they are not necessary to bring the printing press into working condition

– Financing costs are capitalised, as required by IAS 23 *Borrowing Costs*

– The cost of the trial print runs is capitalised on the assumption that the printing press could not otherwise operate at normal levels

Applying a rate of 10% straight line, depreciation of €4,850 ((€53,500 – €5,000) × 10%) will be charged for the year ended 31 December 2x05. This will reduce the net book value of the printing press to €48,650.

At 31 December 2x05 it had become apparent that the carrying value of the printing press may be in excess of its recoverable amount. The following estimated values apply at that date:

- Net selling price €40,000
- Value in use €42,000

Thus the printing press has a recoverable amount of €42,000 (i.e. the higher of its net selling price and its value in use). This is less than the asset's net book value, thus necessitating an impairment write down of €6,650.

The following journal entries will be required during the year ended 31 December 2x05:

	DR €	CR €
Plant & equipment	53,500	
Bank		52,000
Provision for dismantling – SOFP		1,500
(Being capitalisation of the costs of constructing the mini-printing press)		
Depreciation expense – SOCI P/L	4,850	
Accum. depr. plant & machinery		4,850
(Being depreciation charge for year)		
Accumulated depreciation	4,850	
Plant & equipment		4,850
(Being elimination of depreciation at time of impairment of mini-printing press)		
Impairment write-down – SOCI P/L	6,650	
Plant & equipment		6,650
(Being impairment write-down)		

(ii) Subsequent expenditure

The amounts capitalised by Current Issues Limited are analysed as follows:

- *Annual overhaul of printing presses*
  - An entity should not recognise the costs of an asset's day to day servicing as an asset (IAS 16.12). The costs incurred must therefore be expensed to the profit or loss. A case for capitalisation could have been made if it related to a major overhaul, but the annual nature of the

work does not suggest that the work is at the requisite level.

- *Removal of partitioning in factory*
  - Costs shall be recognised as part of a non-current asset if, and only if:

    (i) It is probable that future economic benefits associated with the item will flow to the entity; and

    (ii) The cost of the item can be measured reliably (IAS 16.7).

  - IAS 16.20 also states that the costs of relocating or reorganising part or all of an entity's operations should not be included in the carrying amount of an item of property, plant and equipment.

  - The removal of the partitioning is expected to increase worker productivity, which means that it is probable that future economic benefits will flow to the entity. However, as the removal of partitioning is likely to be construed as the reorganisation of Current Issue Limited's operations, the cost incurred should **not** be capitalised.

  - A valuation of the factory will provide the ultimate test as to whether the removal of the partitioning has increased the asset's value. Should this be the case, then, subject to the company's accounting policy, a revaluation surplus can be recorded.

- *Replacement of lifts*
  - IAS 16.13 states that such expenditure should be capitalised where it complies with the recognition criteria of IAS 16.7 (see above). On the assumption that it does, the cost of replacing the lifts should be capitalised.

  - IAS 16 also requires that the carrying amount of the lift that is replaced should be derecognised (IAS 16.13). The gain or loss should be included in profit or loss. Gains should not be classified as revenue (IAS 16.68).

- *Relocation of printing presses*
  - The costs of reorganising an entity's activities should *not* be capitalised (IAS 16.20 (c)).

- *Extension of warehouse*
  - This expenditure clearly results in an improvement in the non-current asset, with a consequent enhancement of economic benefits. The costs of the extension should therefore be capitalised.

The following journal entry is required to reverse the treatment of amounts which have incorrectly been capitalised:

	DR €	CR €
Expenses – SOCI P/L	330,000	
Non-current assets		330,000

(Being reversal of amounts capitalised relating to the annual overhaul of printing presses, the removal of factory partitioning, and the relocation of printing presses)

(iii)   Revaluation gains

(I)   Office Building

The net book value of the building at 31 December 2x05 was €920,000. The revaluation at 31 December 2x05 will be effected as follows:

	DR €	CR €
Accumulated depreciation	80,000	
Buildings		80,000
Buildings	580,000	
Revaluation surplus – SOCI OCI		580,000*

*Deferred tax is ignored, as per instruction in question.

(II) Factory Building

This represents the reversal in 2x05 of a previously recognised loss. The following journal entries are appropriate (years prior to 2x05 are provided for illustration purposes):

	DR €'000	CR €'000
Buildings	500	
Bank		500
(Being purchase of factory in 2x03)		
Depr. expense – SOCI P/L	10	
Accumulated depr. buildings		10
(Being depr. on factory for 2x03)		
Depr. expense – SOCI P/L	10	
Accumulated depr. buildings		10
(Being depr. on factory for 2x04)		
Accumulated depr. buildings	20	
Buildings		20
(Being elimination of depreciation at time of revaluation of building)		
Write-down of building – SOCI P/L	180	
Buildings		180
(Being write-down of building to €300,000 at 31 December 2x04)		

The building now has a carrying value of €300,000

Depr. expense – SOCI P/L	6.25	
Accumulated depr. buildings		6.25
(Being depr. on factory for 2x05, based on a carrying value of €300,000 and a remaining useful life of 48 years)		

Accumulated depr. buildings   6.25
Buildings   6.25
(Being elimination of depreciation
  at time of revaluation of building)

Buildings   196.25
Revaluation surplus – SOCI OCI   20
Reversal of previous
write-down – SOCI P/L   176.25
(Being reversal of previous write-down)

Thus, the revaluation gain is recognised in the profit or loss only to the extent of the previous impairment loss, as reduced by an adjustment relating to subsequent depreciation (required by IAS 36.117).

i.e. Previous impairment loss – Depreciation adjustment = Gain to be recognised in current yr profit or loss.

€180k – €3.75k** = 176.25 k

**This is the amount by which depreciation fell subsequently (i.e. was not expensed in profit or loss in 2x05) as a result of the write-down in 2x04. This amount is computed as €10k, (i.e. depr. which would have been charged in 2x05 if the asset had not been written down in value) – €6.25k (i.e. actual depr. for 2x05).

(iv)   Revaluation losses

(I)   Land Site
The fall in value of the land site at 31 December 2x05 relates to an impairment in the asset, as its recoverable amount has fallen. This loss in value should be charged to profit or loss for the year ended 31 December 2x05 as follows:

	DR €'000	CR €'000
Impairment write-down – SOCI P/L	100	
Land & buildings		100

(II)   Property

Loss in 2x05 following a previous upward revaluation:
The following journal entries are required (pre-2x05 entries included for illustration purposes):

	DR €'000	CR €'000
Buildings	750	
Bank		750
(Being purchase of property in 2x03)		
Depreciation expense	15	
Accumulated depreciation buildings		15
(Being depreciation of property for 2x03)		
Depreciation expense	15	
Accumulated depreciation buildings		15
(Being depreciation of property for 2x04)		
Accumulated depreciation buildings	30	
Buildings		30
(Being elimination of accumulated depreciation at time of revaluation of building)		
Buildings	280	
Revaluation surplus – SOCI OCI		280*
(Being revaluation of building at 31 December 2x04)		
Depreciation expense	20.8	
Accumulated depreciation buildings		20.8
(Being depreciation of property for 2x05: i.e. €1m × 1/48)		

	DR	CR
Accumulated depreciation buildings	20.8	
Buildings		20.8
(Being elimination of accumulated depreciation at time of revaluation of building)		

Revaluation surplus – SOCI OCI	280	
Buildings		280
(Being set off of loss against revaluation surplus on same asset in 20x5)		

Buildings write-down – SOCI P/L	99.2	
Buildings		99.2
(Being portion of impairment write down charged to profit or loss in 20x5 – i.e. excess of write down over revaluation surplus on the same asset)		

* Deferred tax is ignored, as per instruction in question.

(v) Disposal of land

The following journal entries are required to effect the disposal of the land. Pre-2x05 entries are included for illustration purposes:

	DR €'000	CR €'000
Land	200	
Bank		200
(Being purchase of land in 2x02)		
Land	110	
Revaluation surplus – SOCI OCI		110*
(Being revaluation of land in 2x04)		
Bank	370	
Land		310
Profit on disposal – SOCI P/L		60
(Being profit on disposal in 2x05)		
Revaluation surplus – SOFP	110	
Retained earnings – SOFP		110

(Being realisation of revaluation surplus
  on disposal of land)

*Deferred tax is ignored, as per instruction in question.

(j)   *Accounting Policy Issues*

(i)   Research and development
The Directors have decided that, commencing in 2x05, development costs should be amortised by reference to the expected time horizon of future sales (previously amortised in accordance with expected future sales revenue), as new information indicates that this would better reflect the consumption of the future economic benefits of the development costs.

The question arises as to whether the revised write-off procedure in respect of development costs represents a change in accounting policy.

IAS 8 states that the expected pattern of consumption of the future economic benefits embodied in depreciable assets is an accounting estimate (IAS 8.32). IAS 8 also states that changes in accounting estimates result from new information or new developments, and are therefore not corrections of errors (IAS 8.5).

The decision to amortise development costs over the expected time horizon of future sales is being taken as it would better reflect the consumption of the asset's future economic benefits. This decision is being taken in the light of new information based on past experience. Hence, the change in respect of the amortisation of development costs is a change in accounting estimate.

IAS 8 requires that the effect of a change in accounting estimate shall be recognised prospectively by including it in profit or loss in:

- the period of the change, if the change affects that period only; *or*
- the period of the change and future periods, if the change affects both (IAS 8.36).

(ii) Investment Property
The premises should be reclassified as investment property at 31 December 2x05, and it should be stated at fair value.

The question arises as to whether the revised treatment represents a change in accounting policy. This issue is addressed by IAS 8 *Accounting Policies, Changes in Accounting Estimates and Errors,* which states that the following is **not** a change in accounting policy:

The application of an accounting policy for transactions, other events or conditions that differ in substance from those previously occurring. (IAS 8.16(a))

In the case of the investment property of Current Issues, there is no change in the method of presentation of assets that satisfy the qualifying criteria of IAS 40. Had the premises in question previously satisfied the conditions set by IAS 40, presumably it would have been included in the financial statements as an investment property.

The revised treatment in the 2x05 financial statements results from a condition that differs in substance (i.e. the nature of the asset has changed), rather than from a change in Current Issues' accounting policy. Thus, it does **not** represent a change in accounting policy, and retrospective application does not apply.

The failure to depreciate the premises in 2x03 and 2x04 was, however, an error. If this error is deemed to have been material, it should be corrected retrospectively, in accordance with IAS 8. If not material, no adjustment is required, as the additional depreciation will be offset by the gain on revaluation of the investment property in 2x05.

SOLUTION TO FRONTPAGE GROUP

Rockwell Spate & Co Chartered Accountants

Memorandum

To: **Patrick Queally**

From: **A. Senior**

Date: **20 February 2x06**

Re: **Frontpage Group**

Further to your recent e-mail I have now had the opportunity to review the issues arising in respect of the audit of the Frontpage Group for the year ended 31 December 2x05. I will deal with each issue in turn.

(1) Inventory in Frontpage Limited

(i) *Publishing delay*

The delay in publication of the history book gives rise to a possible NRV issue, as a rival publication is now likely to hit the market before Frontpage Limited.

This can be evaluated as follows:

	€'000
Cost	
Materials	100
Production salaries*	120
Depreciation of equipment	20
	240

*The loss of the illustrations, which had to be re-done in January 2x06, constitutes an abnormal conversion cost, and should be excluded from inventorised costs (IAS 2.16(a)).

General administration and selling and distribution costs should be written off as incurred, and should not be included in the inventory valuation.

	€'000
NRV	
Estimated sales proceeds of history publication	450
Less completion costs and selling & distribution costs:	
Production salaries	(90)
Selling and distribution costs	(220)
Net realisable value	140

The work on the history book, which represents work in progress at 31 December 2x05, should be valued at the lower of cost and net realisable value (IAS 2.9). A journal adjustment is required to re-state inventory to its correct valuation, and this is outlined in Appendix I below.

(ii) **Printing stationery**

Although it may seem reasonable to use LIFO as a method of computing the cost of Frontpage Limited's stationery inventory, its use is not permitted by IAS 2. Thus, it will be necessary to re-state inventory on a FIFO basis (weighted average cost is also permitted by IAS 2).

The old inventory of printing paper should be reviewed for the possibility of physical deterioration, though this seems unlikely as 2x05 is the first year that stationery inventories have been carried, and the reams of paper are kept in a sealed warehouse.

	€'000
LIFO valuation basis	
10,000 reams @ €11.40	114
5,000 reams @ €11.40 × (1.05)	60
	174
FIFO valuation basis	
10,000 reams @ €11.40 × $(1.05)^4$ (note 1)	139
5,000 reams @ €11.40 × $(1.05)^3$ (note 1)	66
	205

(Handwritten top margin:) Increase ASSET → Debit
Decrease Asset → Credit

Note 1: In accordance with IAS 2, inventory should be valued *after* deducting the 5% trade discount (IAS 2.11 and IFRIC November 2004).

Inventories of printing stationery have been included in the financial statements at €174,000 on a LIFO valuation basis. However the use of LIFO is not permitted by IAS 2. It is necessary therefore to employ a FIFO valuation basis, which would give an inventory value of €205,000. Thus a journal adjustment is necessary to increase the inventory value at 31 December 2x05, and this is included in Appendix I below.

(Handwritten right margin:) Disclose, P.Y. → PY adjustme Disclosure policy bigger iss

(iii) *Excess dye*

The excess dye which results from Frontpage Limited's printing process represents a minor by-product, whose cost is not separable from the company's main product. In accordance with IAS 2, the inventories of such by-products, when immaterial, may be measured at net realisable value, and this value is deducted from the cost of the main product (IAS 2.14).

This treatment results in the carrying value of the main product not differing materially from its cost. The following journal entry is required:

	DR €'000	CR €'000
Materials Inventory – SOFP	50	
Cost of sales		50

(Handwritten left margin:) increase inventory ← reduction of costs

(Being inclusion of excess dye as inventory at NRV. An equivalent amount is offset against the production costs of Frontpage Ltd's main product.)

(2) Financing arrangements

- *Bad debt*
  The insolvency of a debtor after the year end is an adjusting event after the reporting period, as outlined in IAS 10.9 (b).

  In this case, a debtor owing the company €500,000 at the year end has gone into liquidation. Frontpage Limited is liable for this entire bad debt, as the factor is in a position to recover its advance of €8 million from the remaining collectible debtors of €9.8 million (€10.3m – €.5m). This is included in the journal adjustments in Appendix I below.

It may also be necessary to reassess the bad debts provision at 31 December 2x05, in view of the liquidation in January 2x06.

- *Presentation in Statement of Financial Position*
  The non-recourse funds of €7m advanced by the factor are non-refundable and, therefore, trade receivables can be reduced by that amount.

  The amount of with-recourse funds received from the factor should continue to be included as a liability in the Statement of Financial Position.

  On the assumption that the bad debts provision will remain at 5% of gross debtors, the presentation in the Statement of Financial Position at 31 December 2x05 can be summarised as follows:

	€'000
Current assets	
Trade and other receivables	2,310*
Current liabilities	
Trade and other payables	7,200**

*Gross amount in statement of financial position – bad debt borne by Frontpage – non-recourse funds from factor – bad debts provision

i.e. €10.3m – €.5m – €7m – €.49m (i.e. €9.8 million × 5%)
= €2.31 million

**Amount per statement of financial position at 31 December 2x05 of €14.2 million, less non-recourse funds advanced by factor of €7m

Disclosure

The bad debt write-off of €500,000, subject to its materiality, should be separately disclosed in the notes to the financial statements, in accordance with IAS 1 (IAS 1.97).

(3) Disposal of shares in Sideissue Limited and related issues

(a) Disposal of shares

Frontpage Limited acquired 30% of the equity shares of Sideissue in 2x02 at a cost of €5 million. Frontpage had representation on the Board of Directors of Sideissue from that date until the disposal of the shares in September 2x05.

As Frontpage held 30% of the shares of Sideissue, it appears to have been in a position to exercise significant influence over that company's financial policies. Sideissue was therefore correctly classified as an associate of Frontpage (IAS 28.5). On this basis, it was accounted for under the equity basis of accounting in the consolidated financial statements of the Frontpage Group.

The profit/loss on disposal of the shares in Sideissue will be recorded as follows:

(I) Financial statements of Frontpage Limited

The profit or loss on disposal of the shares held in Sideissue should be computed as follows:

	€'000
Proceeds of sale	9,000
Cost of shares	(5,000)
Profit on disposal	4,000

As this amount is material, it should be disclosed separately, either in the Statement of Comprehensive Income or the notes of Frontpage Limited, in accordance with IAS 1 *Presentation of Financial Statements* (IAS 1.97).

The following journal will be required in the financial statements of Frontpage Limited to record the disposal:

	DR €'000	CR €'000
Bank	9,000	
Investment in Sideissue		5,000
Profit on disposal – SOCI P/L		4,000

(II) Group Financial Statements
The profit or loss on disposal of the shares held in Sideissue should be computed as follows:

	€'000	€'000
Proceeds of sale		9,000
Less carrying amount of Sideissue at date of disposal (IAS 28.22 (b))		
Acquisition cost of shares	5,000	
Frontpage Limited's share of post-acquisition profits brought forward at 1 January 2x05 (€7 million – €4 million) × 30%	900	
Frontpage Limited's share of retained profits of Sideissue for the 9 months ended 30 September 2x05 (€2 million – €600,000) × 30%	420	
		(6,320)
Profit on disposal		2,680

As the profit on disposal is a material amount, it should be separately disclosed in the Consolidated Statement of Comprehensive Income of the Frontpage Group, or in the notes, in accordance with IAS 1 *Presentation of Financial Statements* (IAS 1.97).

The following journal will be required in the financial statements of the Group to record the disposal:

	DR €'000	CR €'000
Bank	9,000	
Investment in Sideissue		6,320
Profit on disposal – SOCI P/L		2,680

(b) *Inter-company sales*
In the nine months ended 30 September 2x05, Backpage Limited recorded sales of €900,000 to Sideissue. Backpage Limited is a subsidiary of Frontpage Limited, and Sideissue was an associate of Frontpage up to the time of its disposal.

Backpage and Frontpage are defined as related parties by IAS 24. As the amount of inter-company sales is material, details should be disclosed as follows:

- Description of the relationship between them (Subsidiary and Associate of Frontpage)
- The amounts involved (Sales for the nine months ended 30 September 2x05)
- Any other elements of the transaction necessary for an understanding of the financial statements
- The amounts due to or from the related parties at end of the reporting period, and provisions for doubtful debts due from such parties at that date (IAS 24.17).

Disclosure will be required in the following financial statements:

(i)   *Group financial statements*
Disclosure is required as a subsidiary and an associate are defined as related parties by IAS 24.

(ii)   *Financial statements of Sideissue Limited*
Disclosure is required.

(iii) *Financial statements of Backpage Limited*
Disclosure is required.

(4) Construction of office building

(i)   *Reinstatement of costs written off*
Where assets, other than goodwill, suffer an impairment in value, IAS 36 *Impairment of Assets*, requires the impairment write-down to be reversed if there has been a change in the estimates used to determine the asset's recoverable amount since the last impairment loss was recognised (IAS 36.114).
It is a requirement of IAS 36, however, that the carrying amount of an asset attributable to a reversal of an impairment loss shall not exceed the carrying amount that would have been determined (net of depreciation)

had no impairment loss been recognised for the asset in previous years (IAS 36.117).

This applies in the case of Backpage Limited, as the building was available for use in November 2x03. IAS 16 states that depreciation should be charged during periods that an asset is idle (IAS 16.55). Thus, depreciation would have been higher had the impairment loss not been written off to profit or loss.

Depreciation which would otherwise have been charged is calculated as follows:

€'000

Years ended 31 December 2x03, and
31 December 2x04 (€1 million × 2% × 2 years)   40

IAS 36 also states that any increase in the carrying value of an asset above the carrying amount that would have been determined (net of depreciation) had no impairment loss been recognised for the asset in prior years is a revaluation (IAS 36.118).

Thus, the impairment write-back to profit or loss in 2x05 is restricted and is limited to €960,000. An adjusting journal entry is required, as Backpage credited the entire reversal of €1 million to profit or loss. This adjustment is outlined in Appendix I below.

(ii)   Capitalisation of borrowing costs
The Board of Backpage capitalised borrowing costs incurred in respect of the construction of the office building. IAS 23 *Borrowing Costs* restricts the capitalisation of borrowing costs to amounts incurred during the period of construction. Thus, only the interest incurred between the commencement of construction (1 January 2x03) and the point of completion (30 November 2x03) can be capitalised.

A journal adjustment is required to reverse the amount capitalised in 2x05 relating to the period after 30 November 2x03 (i.e. €200,000). This adjustment is outlined in Appendix I below.

It will also be necessary to allow for depreciation on the amount of borrowing costs capitalised relating to the 2x03 construction period. This is computed as €6,000 (i.e. €100,000 × 2% × 3 years). See journal adjustment in Appendix I.

(5) Legal and miscellaneous issues

(i) *Legal action*

As there has been no further development of the legal action threatened by the rival publishing group, there may be only a remote possibility that legal action will be taken against Frontpage Limited. This viewpoint would seem to be supported by the fact that there has been no evidence in writing that the publishing group intends to proceed with its claim. Legal advice could, if necessary, be sought to confirm that John Walker is correct in this regard.

Should it transpire that there is more than a remote possibility of a claim against Frontpage being successful, details of the contingent loss should be disclosed by way of note in the financial statements, in accordance with IAS 37 *Provisions, Contingent Liabilities and Contingent Assets* (IAS 37.28). If it is probable that a claim against the company would be likely to succeed, provision should be made for any probable loss (IAS 37.14).

On the basis of the available evidence, it would not seem appropriate to recognise a provision, or make any disclosures relating to the threat of legal action, at this stage.

The possible counter-claim which John Walker has mentioned should be separately assessed. At this stage it does not seem likely to arise, and it should not be recognised or disclosed in the financial statements.

(ii) *Artistic work*

IAS 16 *Property, Plant and Equipment* permits entities to use either the cost model or the revaluation model. It is clear that Frontpage has used the cost model in accounting for the painting. The net book value of €8,000 at 31 December is therefore a correct valuation, and no adjustment is required in the 2x05 financial statements.

Thomas Walker is a close relative of John Walker, who is a member of the key management personnel of Frontpage. Margin Limited is therefore a related party of Frontpage, as that company is controlled by Thomas Walker.

The sale of the painting would therefore be identified by IAS 24 *Related Party Disclosures* as being a related party transaction

(IAS 24.9). Thus, details of the transaction should be disclosed as follows:

- Description of the relationship between the parties (company controlled by close family member of key management personnel in Frontpage);
- The amounts involved (sale of painting for €350,000, which had a market value of €700,000);
- Any other elements of the transaction necessary for an understanding of the financial statements;
- The amounts due to or from the related parties at the end of the reporting period, and provisions for doubtful debts due from such parties at that date (IAS 24.17).

Disclosure should be made in the 2x06 Group Financial Statements, as the transaction involving the painting took place between a member of the Group (i.e. Frontpage Limited) and a party to whom the group is related (i.e. Margin Limited).

Disclosure is also required in the financial statements of Frontpage Limited.

The following journal entry will be required in the 2x06 financial statements of the Frontpage Group:

	DR €'000	CR €'000
Bank	350	
P, P + E		8
Profit on disposal of asset – SOCI P/L		342

(6) Deferred Tax

Deferred tax provision required at 31 December 2x05:

	€'000
Accelerated capital allowances (note 1)	500
Pension costs accrued (note 2)	(300)
Deposit interest prepayment (note 3)	80
Development costs (note 4)	250
Net temporary taxable difference requiring a deferred tax provision	530

Deferred tax provision required at 25%
(i.e. at the tax rate currently enacted)   133
Add deferred tax provision on land (note 5)   100
Deferred tax provision required at 31 December 2x05   233
Less deferred tax provision at 31 December 2x04   (100)

Increase in deferred tax provision at 31 December 2x05   133

Note 1: NBV of plant and machinery €1.4 million, less tax base of €900,000. This is a taxable temporary difference of €500,000.

Note 2: Pension costs are allowed for taxation when paid. Therefore the €300,000, which has already been charged in Frontpage Limited's Statement of Comprehensive Income, will be allowed for taxation purposes when it is paid. The accrual therefore represents a deductible temporary difference, as the carrying value of the accrual at 31 December 2x05 was €300,000 and its tax base was zero.

Note 3: Deposit interest is taxed on receipt. The deposit interest prepayment therefore represents a taxable temporary difference. Its carrying value at 31 December 2x05 was €80,000 and its tax base was zero.

Note 4: Development costs are tax deductible when paid. There is a taxable temporary difference at 31 December 2x05, as the carrying value of the asset is €250,000 at that date, and its tax base is zero.

Note 5: Taxable Temporary Difference on land:
Frontpage Limited has land which has been revalued by €500,000. At a capital gains tax rate of 20%, this will give rise to an expected capital gains tax liability of €100,000 (i.e. €500,000 @ 20%). This was a taxable temporary difference at 31 December 2x05, as the carrying value of the asset was €500,000 more than its tax base.

Appendix I

Journal entries in Group Financial Statements:

	DR €'000	CR €'000
Cost of sales	250	
Inventory – SOFP		250

(Being adjustment to reduce work in progress
 at 31 December 2x05 to net realisable value)

Inventory – SOFP	31	
Cost of sales		31

(Being adjustment to restate inventories of
printing stationery to a FIFO valuation basis
at 31 December 2x05)

Materials Inventory – SOFP	50	
Cost of sales		50

(Being inclusion of excess dye as inventory at
NRV. An equivalent amount is offset against
the production costs of Frontpage Ltd's main
product.)

Bad debts expense – SOCI P/L	500	
Trade receivables		500

(Being liquidation of customer in January
2x06, all of which is borne by Frontpage Ltd)

Increase in prov. for bad debts – SOCI P/L	240	
Provision for bad debts – SOFP		240

(Being increase in bad debts provision at
31 December 2x05)

Impairment loss reversal – SOCI P/L	40	
Revaluation surplus – SOCI OCI		40

(Being restriction of impairment write-back
by Backpage in 2x05)

Finance costs – SOCI P/L	200	
Buildings		200

(Being restriction of capitalisation of borrowing
costs to the period of construction of the office
building by Backpage Ltd)

Depreciation expense	6	
Accumulated depreciation of buildings		6

(Being depreciation on amount of finance costs capitalised:
€100,000 × 2% × 3 years)

Revaluation surplus – SOCI OCI	100*	
Deferred tax – SOCI P/L	33	
Deferred tax provision – SOFP		133
(Being increase in deferred tax provision		
at 31 December 2x05)		

*It should be noted that, as the revaluation surplus is recorded in other compre-
hensive income, so also should the deferred tax that relates to that surplus.

SOLUTION TO HARDCOURT GROUP

Comerford Lane & Co. Chartered Accountants

Memorandum

To: Beatrice Lambe

From: A. Senior

Date: 26 February 2x06

Re: Hardcourt Group

Further to your recent e-mail I have now had the opportunity to review the issues arising in respect of the audit of the Hardcourt Group for the year ended 31 December 2x05. I will deal with each issue in turn.

(1) Acquisition of Claycourt Limited

IFRS 3 *Business Combinations* requires that an acquirer shall recognise an acquiree's identifiable assets at their acquisition date fair values (IFRS 3.18).

Fair value is defined as "… the price that would be received to sell an asset in an orderly transaction between market participants" (IFRS 13, Appendix A).

(i) Inventory

Prior to the work in progress inventory of Claycourt Limited being available for sale, it will be necessary to deduct the completion costs. The fair value is therefore calculated as follows:

	€'000
Selling price	400
Less completion costs	(70)
Fair value as per IFRS 3	330

It will therefore be necessary to reduce the value of Claycourt Limited's inventory from its book value of €500,000 to its fair value of €330,000.

(ii) *Due diligence costs*
IFRS 3 requires that the acquirer shall account for acquisition-related costs as expenses in the periods in which the costs are incurred (IFRS 3.53). The due diligence costs therefore have been correctly charged to profit or loss of Hardcourt Limited in the year ended 31 December 2x05.

(iii) *Quoted investments*
Quoted investments should be valued at market price, which in this case is €800,000.

(iv) *Intra-group sales*
IFRS 10 requires that intragroup transactions be eliminated in full (IFRS 10, B86). Profits and losses resulting from intragroup transactions that are recognised in assets, such as inventory, should also be eliminated in full (IFRS 10, B86).

(v) *Goodwill arising on the acquisition of Claycourt Limited:*

	€'000	€'000
Consideration paid		8,500
Non-controlling interest* (€7,230k × 15%)		1,085
		9,585
Less fair value of identifiable net assets acquired:		
Book value	7,000	
Reduction in value of inventory	(170)	
Fair value premium of quoted investments	500	
Deferred tax on premium @ 20%	(100)	

	(7,230)
Goodwill arising on acquisition	2,355

*IFRS 3 states that an acquirer shall measure any non-controlling interest in an acquiree either at fair value or at the non-controlling interest's proportionate share of the acquiree's identifiable net assets (IFRS 3.19). The latter method of measurement is adopted in this solution, in accordance with the group's policy.

(vi)   *Journal entries*

Financial Statements of the Group:

	DR €'000	CR €'000
Net assets	7,230	
Goodwill on acquisition	2,355	
Bank		8,500
Non-controlling interest (15%)		1,085
(Being acquisition of Claycourt Limited)		
Cost of sales*	40	
Inventory		40
(Being elimination of unrealised intra-group profit on inventory: i.e. €200k × 1/5)		
Deferred tax asset – SOFP	12	
Deferred tax credit – SOCI P/L*		12
(Being deferred tax impact on elimination of unrealised inter-company profit on inventory: deductible difference of €40k × 30%)		

*NCI will be charged/credited with their share of these adjustments when profit for the year in the consolidated SOCI is divided between owners of the parent and NCI.

Financial Statements of Hardcourt Limited:

	DR €'000	CR €'000
Investment at cost	8,500	
Bank		8,500
(Being consideration paid for acquisition of Claycourt Limited)		

(vii) *Disclosure issues*

Group Financial Statements – General Disclosures

IFRS 3 requires that an acquirer shall disclose information that enables users of its financial statements to evaluate the nature and financial effect of a business combination that occurs during the current reporting period (IFRS 3.59).

Related party disclosures

Group Financial Statements

IAS 24 classifies a parent company and its subsidiary as being related parties (IAS 24.9). Inter-company sales in the post-acquisition period will be cancelled in the group financial statements, and therefore no disclosure issues arise.

Financial Statements of Hardcourt Limited

Hardcourt Limited will be required to provide details of transactions with Claycourt for the six months ended 31 December 2x05.

Financial Statements of Claycourt Limited

The financial statements of Claycourt Limited should disclose the following information:

- the fact that Hardcourt Limited is the parent company of Claycourt Limited
- sales to Hardcourt Limited for the 6 months ended 31 December 2x05
- the amount of outstanding balances.

(2) Revaluation of land

The following journal entries would have been made at the time of the previous revaluation:

	DR €'000	CR €'000
Land	500	
Revaluation surplus – SOCI OCI		500
(Being revaluation of land from €1m to €1.5m)		
Revaluation surplus – SOCI OCI	100	
Deferred tax provision – SOFP		100
(Being deferred tax on revaluation surplus)		

The subsequent loss in value of the land, resulting from the rezoning decision, is an impairment as defined by IAS 36 *Impairment of Assets*. It should first be offset against the previous revaluation surplus on the land, with the excess being charged in profit or loss for the year ended 31 December 2x05 (IAS 36.60).

	DR €'000	CR €'000
Revaluation surplus – SOCI OCI	400	
Deferred tax provision – SOFP	100	
Impairment write-down – SOCI P/L	300	
Land		800
(Being impairment write-down of land)		

A deferred tax asset may possibly arise in respect of the impairment write-down of land. This would occur if the impairment write-down of €300,000 can be offset against capital gains arising on other assets within the Hardcourt Group. The maximum amount of the deferred tax asset would be €60,000 (i.e. €300,000 × 20%).

(3) Restructuring

A detailed restructuring plan has been drawn up in respect of the closure of the timberland division, and details have been announced to the staff.

Consequently certain restructuring costs should be recognised as a provision in accordance with IAS 37 *Provisions, Contingent Liabilities and Contingent Assets*.

(i) *Redundancy costs*

A provision should be made, in accordance with IAS 37, for redundancy costs which are likely to be incurred in the restructuring.

It is certain that redundancy costs of €800,000 will be incurred. This amount should be provided for at 31 December 2x05.

Additionally, it is possible that further redundancy settlements of €200,000 may have to be paid. This will be classified as a contingent liability under IAS 37, and details should be disclosed (IAS 37.28).

(ii) *Operating losses*

Operating losses of €600,000 are expected to be incurred by the timberland division in the five months ending 31 May 2x06. IAS 37 states that provisions should *not* be recognised for future operating losses (IAS 37.63). This treatment is stipulated as future operating losses do not meet the definition of a liability, which requires a present obligation arising from past events.

IAS 37 also states however that, where an entity has an onerous contract, the present obligation under the contract should be recognised and measured as a provision (IAS 37.66). Although the timberland division is closing, contractual commitments are in place to continue to service customers until 31 May 2x06. On the assumption that this commitment can be verified, it appears to constitute an onerous contract, and the costs of fulfilling it should be provided, as it gives rise to a present obligation arising from past events. Thus, to the extent that the operating losses for the first five months of 2x06 relate to contractual commitments to customers, a provision should be made for this amount at 31 December 2x05.

Alternatively, should the costs of breaching the contractual commitments with customers be less than the operating losses that will be incurred in fulfilling the contract, the former should instead be provided in accordance with IAS 37.

(iii)   *Discontinued operation*

IFRS 5 defines a discontinued operation as "a component of an entity that either has been disposed of, or is classified as held for sale and:

- represents a separate major line of business or geographical area of operations
- is part of a single co-ordinated plan to dispose of a separate major line of business or geographical area of operations, *or*
- is a subsidiary acquired exclusively with a view to resale" (IFRS 5.32).

The timerberland division clearly has not been disposed of as yet. Consequently, to be classified as a discontinued operation, the assets of the division would have to be classified as held for sale. For this to be the case, an asset or disposal group must be available for immediate sale in its present condition (IFRS 5.7). As operating activities must continue until the 31 May 2x06, clearly this condition is not satisfied at the 31 December 2x05. The timberland division must therefore be classified as a continuing operation for the year ended 31 December 2x05.

The decision to close the timberland division should be disclosed in the financial statements.

(4) Land

IFRS 5 *Non-current Assets Held for Sale and Discontinued Operations* states that an entity shall classify an asset as held for sale if its carrying amount will be recovered principally through a sale transaction rather than through continuing use (IFRS 5.6).
For this to be the case:

- the asset must be available for immediate sale in its present condition;
- the sale must be highly probable;
- the transfer is to be completed within one year (IFRS 5.7–5.8).

The land site that is surplus to requirements appears to satisfy the above criteria, and it should therefore be regarded as a non-current asset held for sale. The land should:

- be shown separately in the statement of financial position as an asset held for sale
- be valued at the lower of carrying value and fair value less costs to sell.

If the land were a depreciable asset, it should not be depreciated any further after it has been classified as held for sale.

The following information is available in respect of the land:

- Fair Value   €2 million
- Carrying Value   €1.7 million
- Selling Costs   €30k
- Cost   €800k

The following journal entries are applicable:

	DR €'000	CR €'000
Property, Plant & Equipment	800	
Bank		800
(Being original purchase of land)		
Property, Plant & Equipment	900	
Revaluation surplus – SOCI OCI		900
(Being revaluation of land to €1.7m under the revaluation model of IAS 16)		
Revaluation surplus – SOCI OCI	180	
Deferred tax provision – SOFP		180
(Being tax @ 20% on revaluation surplus)		
Property, Plant & Equipment	300	
Revaluation surplus – SOCI OCI		300
(Being revaluation of land by €300k under the revaluation model of IAS 16, prior to being re-classified as held for sale, in accordance with IFRS 5.18)		

Revaluation surplus – SOCI OCI	60	
Deferred tax provision – SOFP		60
(Being tax @ 20% on revaluation surplus)		

Non-current asset held for sale	2,000	
Property, Plant & Equipment		2,000
(Being transfer of asset in accordance with IFRS 5)		

At the point that the asset is transferred to non-current assets held for sale, a further adjustment is necessary as the fair value less costs to sell (€1.97m) is less than the asset's carrying value of €2m (IFRS 5.15).

Revaluation surplus – SOCI OCI*	30	
Provision for selling expenses – SOFP		30
(Being provision for selling expenses of asset held for sale)		

Deferred tax provision – SOFP	6	
Revaluation surplus – SOCI OCI		6

(Being reduction of deferred tax provision, on the assumption that the selling expenses are deductible in computing the chargeable gain on disposal of the land)

*IFRS 5 does not provide guidance as to whether the selling costs should be charged to profit or loss or other comprehensive income when a revaluation surplus exists in respect of an asset. In this solution, the selling costs are offset against the revaluation surplus.

The balance on revaluation surplus will remain until the asset is sold, at which point it will be transferred to retained earnings (IAS 16.41).

(5) Capital Grants

Government grants should not be recognised until there is reasonable assurance that:

- the entity will comply with the grant conditions
- the grant will be received (IAS 20.7).

This clearly implies that government grants should be recognised once the above conditions are satisfied. This view is supported in the IASB's Conceptual

Framework document, which states that income should be recognised when an increase in future economic benefits, related to an increase in an asset, has arisen and can be reliably measured (Paragraph 4.47).

It is not permissible therefore to account for capital grants on a cash receipts basis. Thus, the change to an accruals basis for recognising the grants in the financial statements is the correction of an error. If it is considered to be a *material* error, IAS 8 requires that a retrospective correction be made (IAS 8.42). Otherwise, the correction will be made in the current period only.

In respect of the grant commitments in place at 31 December 2x05, on the assumption that there is reasonable assurance of the grant conditions being complied with, the following journal adjustment will be required:

	DR €'000	CR €'000
Receivables	200	
Deferred income – SOFP		200

Disclosure issues

Machinery was sold by Hardcourt Limited to Claycourt Limited in November 2x05. As these companies are related parties (Claycourt is a subsidiary of Hardcourt), IAS 24 requires the following disclosure:

Financial statements of the Group

No disclosure will be required in the group financial statements, as this transaction will be cancelled on consolidation.

Individual financial statements of Claycourt Limited and separate financial statements of Hardcourt Limited

The following information should be disclosed in the financial statements of Claycourt Limited and Hardcourt Limited:

- Description of the relationship between the related parties (Parent and subsidiary);
- Description of the transactions (Sale of machinery);
- The amounts involved (Value of machinery sold);
- The amount of any outstanding balances and provisions for doubtful debts relating thereto;
- Any other elements of the transaction necessary for an understanding of the financial statements (IAS 24.17).

SOLUTION TO HEALTHFIRST GROUP

Lantry Mansfield & Co.

Memorandum

To: **Susan Gilmartin**

From: **A. Senior**

Date: **24 February 2x06**

Re: **Healthfirst Group**

Further to our recent meeting I have now had the opportunity to review the issues arising in respect of the audit of the Healthfirst Group for the year ended 31 December 2x05. I will deal with each issue in turn.

(1) Goodwill arising on the acquisition of Scanright Limited

Goodwill on acquisition will be computed as follows at 1 April 2x05:

	€'000	Parent €'000	NCI €'000
Cost of investment		6,500	
Non-controlling interests (€6,500,000 x 15/85)			1,147
Book value of identifiable net assets acquired at 1 April 2x05	4,800		
Premium on valuation of land holdings	800		

Deferred tax provision			
on premium @ 20%	(160)		
Reduction in value of inventory	(95)		
	(5,345)	(4,543)	(802)
Goodwill arising on consolidation		1,957	345

Total goodwill arising on the acquisition of Scanright is €2,302,000. Of this amount, €1,957,000 relates to the owners of Healthfirst, and €345,000 relates to NCI.

(2) Intragroup sales

IFRS 10 *Consolidated Financial Statements* requires that intragroup transactions should be eliminated in full (IFRS 10, B86). Profits and losses resulting from intragroup transactions that are recognised in assets, such as inventory, should also be eliminated in full (IFRS 10, B86).

In respect of the intra-group sales by Scanright to Healthfirst, the profit should be eliminated to the extent that the goods have not been resold outside of the Group. Thus the amount of profit that should be eliminated can be computed as follows:

€960,000 × 20% (percentage of goods still held by Healthfirst)
× 20% (margin of profit) = €38,400.

The following journal entry will be required in the group financial statements to effect this elimination of profit:

	DR €'000	CR €'000
Cost of sales	38.4*	
Inventory (SOFP)		38.4
Deferred tax asset – SOFP	9.6	
Deferred tax credit – SOCI P/L		9.6*

(Being deferred tax asset arising – i.e. €38.4k x 25%)

*NCI will be charged/credited with 15% of these amounts, when the group profit for the year (in the consolidated SOCI) is divided between the owners of Healthfirst and the NCI.

IAS 24 *Related Party Disclosures* requires that disclosure be made of related party transactions. As there is a parent/subsidiary relationship, Healthfirst Limited is deemed to be a related party of Scanright Limited (IAS 24.9). Disclosure of intra-group sales will be required as follows:

(i)   *Group Financial Statements*   Eliminated → no requirement.
      Inter-company sales between Healthfirst and Scanright which occurred in the post-acquisition period will be cancelled on consolidation, and therefore disclosure will not be required in the Group financial statements.

(ii) *Financial statements of Healthfirst and Scanright*   individual Accounts
      Both companies will be required to provide details of inter-company sales as follows, in accordance with IAS 24.17:

      - the nature of the relationship between the parties;
      - a description of the transactions;
      - the amounts involved;
      - amounts of outstanding balances;
      - provisions for doubtful debts.

(3) Deferred Taxation

IAS 12 requires that deferred tax be provided on almost all temporary differences. Thus the amount of deferred tax that should be provided by the Healthfirst Group at 31 December 2x05 can be computed as follows:

		€'000
Deposit interest:		
Carrying value in financial statements	€50k	
Tax base	–	
Taxable temporary difference @ 31 December 2x05		50
Plant and machinery:		
NBV of plant and machinery @ 31 Dec. 2x05	€2m	
Tax WDV of plant and machinery @ 31 Dec. 2x05	€1.4m	
Taxable temporary difference @ 31 December 2x05		600
Development costs:		
Carrying value in financial statements	€800k	
Tax base	–	
Taxable temporary difference		800

Intra-group sales (see 2 above):

Carrying value of inventory in financial statements	–	
Tax base	38.4k	
Deductible temporary difference		(38.4)
Net taxable temporary differences		1,411.6
Deferred tax @ 25%		352.9 ✓
Deferred tax on revaluation gain @ 20% (500)		100
Deferred tax provision required @ 31 December 2x05		452.9
Less existing provision		(100.0)
Increase in deferred tax provision at 31 December 2x05		352.9

The following journal entries will be required in the financial statements of the Healthfirst Group at 31 December 2x05.

	DR €'000	CR €'000
Deferred tax charge – SOCI P/L	252.9	
Deferred tax provision – SOFP		252.9

(Being increase in deferred tax provision on items subject to income tax @ 25%)

	DR €'000	CR €'000
Deferred tax charge – SOCI OCI	100	
Deferred tax provision – SOFP		100

(Being deferred tax provision in respect of the revaluation of land & buildings)

Disclosures

- Major components of the tax expense
- Aggregate current and deferred tax relating to items taken to equity
- Explanation of the relation between tax expense and accounting profit/loss
- Explanation of changes in tax rates
- Amount (and dates) of any deductible temporary differences unrecognised
- Aggregate of temporary differences relating to investments for which no deferred tax liability is recognised

- For each type of temporary difference, deferred tax assets and liabilities recognised, not recognised, and the movement recognised in the income statement (IAS 12.79–12.81)

(4) Investment property

IAS 40 *Investment Property* requires that, if a building is to qualify as investment property, it must not be occupied by the owner (IAS 40.9 (c)). Thus, this building must be re-classified as land and buildings with effect from 1 January 2x05, and the asset transferred out of investment property at its fair value (IAS 40.60).

While this is a change in presentation of the building in the financial statements, it relates to an alteration in the nature of the asset, rather than a change in the accounting policy of the Healthfirst Group. Thus, this is *not* a change in accounting policy (as defined by IAS 8) and retrospective application is not required.

The following journal entry will be required at 31 December 2x05:

	DR €'000	CR €'000
Land and buildings	1,300	
Investment property		1,300
(Being re-classification of the investment property in 2x05)		
Depreciation expense – SOCI P/L	26	
Accumulated depreciation buildings		26
(Being depreciation on the building @ 2% p.a. straight line for y/e 31 December 2x05)		

(5) Sale of franchise

IAS 38 *Intangible Assets* requires that an intangible asset should be derecognised on disposal, and that the gain or loss should be determined as the difference between the net disposal proceeds and the carrying amount of the asset (IAS 38.113).

IAS 38 also states that the gain/loss should be recognised in profit or loss, but should not be classified as revenue (IAS 38.113).

Thus, the following journal entry will be required in respect of the sale of the franchise on 1 November 2x05:

	DR €'000	CR €'000
Revenue – SOCI P/L	2,273	
Trade receivables		2,273
(Being reversal of sales entry made by Suretime Ltd – i.e. $2.5m/1.1)		
Trade receivables	2,273	
Franchise – SOFP		1,000
Profit on disposal of franchise – SOCI P/L		1,273
(Being disposal of franchise on 1 November 2x05)		
Bank/Financial Asset	2,381	
Trade receivables		2,273
Foreign currency gain – SOCI P/L		108
(Being receipt of sales proceeds on 20 December 2x05 – i.e. $2.5m/1.05)		

The profit on sale will, subject to materiality, be disclosed separately in the statement of comprehensive income or the notes of Suretime Limited, and in the consolidated financial statements of the Healthfirst Group (IAS 1.97).

At 31 December 2x05, the $2.5 million held on deposit is a monetary asset, and it should be translated into € at the exchange rate prevailing at the end of the reporting period (IAS 21.23). Thus the following journal entry will be required:

	DR €'000	CR €'000
Bank/Financial Asset	119	
Foreign currency gain – SOCI P/L		119

(Being gain on translation of funds held in $ bank a/c on 31 December 2x05: i.e. (2.5m/1) − (2.5m/1.05))

The exchange rate prevailing on 15 February 2x06 is a non-adjusting event after the reporting period, as defined by IAS 10, and it should not be included in the financial statements for the year ended 31 December 2x05.

[handwritten margin note: on adjusting event: does not provide additional information in relation to an event NOT occured before yr/end.]

SOLUTION TO MAINPART GROUP

Mr Patrick Hartson
Chairman,
Mainpart Holdings Limited,
Main Street,
Maintown

28 February 2x06

Report on accounting issues in respect of 2x05 Audit

Dear Mr Hartson,

Further to our recent discussions, we enclose a copy of our report for the Board, which sets out the appropriate accounting treatment and disclosure requirements regarding various matters which have arisen in respect of the 2x05 audit of the Mainpart Group companies.

We look forward to discussing these issues with you in detail.

Yours sincerely,

A. Bitpart
Witherspoon, Holt & Co., Chartered Accountants

(1) Construction of Building

(a) *Costs to be capitalised*

IAS 16 *Property, Plant and Equipment* requires that property, plant and equipment should initially be measured at cost (IAS 16.15). Cost comprises an asset's:

- purchase price;
- any costs directly attributable* to bringing the asset to the location and condition necessary for it to be capable of operating in the manner intended by management;
- the initial estimate of dismantling and removing the item (IAS 16.16).

*Directly attributable costs are the incremental costs that would have been avoided if the asset had not been constructed or acquired.

The following costs should be capitalised in respect of the construction of the new factory premises:

		€'000
Site preparation costs		100
External labour costs (excluding 'abnormal' costs caused by the industrial dispute)		600
Materials (exclusive of VAT and trade discount)		1,295.45
Production overheads		
– Staff recruited for project	100	
– Salary of safety officers	140	
– Other variable overheads	80	
		320
Interest costs (Note 1)		240
Total cost of building		2,555.45

The amount of costs capitalised must therefore be reduced by €774,550, necessitating the following journal adjustment:

	DR €'000	CR €'000
Expenses – SOCI P/L	774.55	
Buildings		774.55

Note 1: Interest Costs

Restrict to exclude strike period during which the interest cost was a holding cost, and not a cost of production (IAS 23.20).

$$\text{Interest to be capitalised} = €300,000 \times \frac{8 \text{ months}}{10 \text{ months}}$$

$$= €240,000$$

The investment income of €12,000 earned during the strike period should be included in profit or loss for the period.

Note 2: Excluded costs

IAS 16 does not permit the capitalisation of the following costs:

	€'000
General management – not directly attributable	100
Re-design costs – 'abnormal' cost	170
Location map & brochure – not a production cost	10
Security personnel recruitment – occurs after construction period	20
Official opening luncheon – not a production cost	30

(b) *Related Party Disclosure*

IAS 24 *Related Party Disclosures* requires the disclosure of transactions with related parties. The standard identifies an investor and associate as related parties (IAS 24.9). Mainpart Limited holds 22% of the shares in Small Part Limited who supplied the labour for the construction of the building. Should Mainpart be in a position to exercise significant influence over Small Part Limited, the two companies would therefore be related parties under IAS 24. On the assumption that this is the case, the following disclosures are required:

Disclosures required in the Group Financial Statements and Financial Statements of Mainpart Limited and Small Part:

- Description of the relationship between the parties (investing company and associate);
- Description of the transaction (Provision of external labour for construction of factory premises);
- The amounts involved (Cost of labour supplied);
- The amount of outstanding balances and provisions for doubtful debts related thereto;
- Any other elements of the transaction necessary for an understanding of the financial statements (IAS 24.17).

(2) Disposal of Subsidiary

(a) *Profit on Disposal*

(i) Separate financial statements of Mainpart Limited

The profit on disposal of an asset is the difference between net sales proceeds and the carrying amount at the time of disposal. This can be computed as follows:

	€'000
Net sales proceeds	32,000
Carrying amount (i.e. cost × 90%)	(19,800)
Profit on disposal	12,200

The draft financial statements of Mainpart Limited have incorrectly computed the profit on disposal as being €10 million (i.e. €32 million – €22 million). This error is due to the fact that the entire investment has been eliminated from the statement of financial positions, even though a 10% shareholding is still retained. The following journal adjustment will therefore be required:

	€'000	€'000
Investment @ cost	2,200	
Profit on disposal – SOCI P/L		2,200

(ii) Group Financial Statements

If a parent loses control of a subsidiary, in accordance with IFRS 10, it should:

- derecognise the assets and liabilities of the former subsidiary from the consolidated statement of financial position

- recognise any investment retained in the former subsidiary at its fair value at the date when control is lost

- recognise the gain or loss associated with the loss of control (IFRS 10.25).

In respect of the disposal of 90% of Subpart Limited, this is represented as follows:

	€'000
Consideration received	32,000
Investment retained at fair value	3,500
	35,500

Less:

Goodwill at 1 July 2x05 relating to the acquisition of Subpart	2,000
Assets less liabilities of the subsidiary at their carrying amounts at the date that control is lost	26,000
Profit on disposal of Subpart Limited – Consolidated SOCI P/L	7,500

Subpart Limited's results should be included in the Group Financial Statements up to the date of disposal – i.e. 1 July 2x05 (IFRS 10.20). In accordance with IAS 1, the profit on disposal should be separately disclosed in the current year's statement of comprehensive income or in the notes of Mainpart Limited **and** of the Group (IAS 1.97).

(b) Disclosure issues

(i) Disposal

- A component of an entity is defined as *Operations and cash flows that can be clearly distinguished, operationally and for financial reporting purposes, from the rest of the entity* (IFRS 5 Appendix A). It is clear that Subpart Limited, being a separate legal entity, qualifies as a component of the Mainpart Group.

- A discontinued operation is a *component of an entity* that meets the conditions outlined in IFRS 5.32. To be classified as a discontinued operation, a component of an entity must be held for sale, or already disposed of, and meet one of the following criteria:

  - It must represent a major line of business or geographical area of operations;
  - It must be part of a single co-ordinated plan to dispose of a separate major line of business or geographical area of operations;
  - It must be a subsidiary acquired exclusively with a view to resale.

The net assets of Subpart were €26 million on the date that Mainpart lost control of the subsidiary. The total net assets of the Mainpart Group amounted to €62.25 million in the draft financial statements at 31 December 2x05. It is clear therefore that Subpart Limited represents a major line of business in the context of the group, and the disposal of 90% of that company constitutes a discontinued operation.

Disclosures required:
- *On the face of the statement of comprehensive income:*
  A single amount, being the total of the after tax profit or loss of the discontinued operation, and the after tax gain or loss from disposing of the assets comprising the discontinued operation (IFRS 5.33(a)).

- *In the notes or on the face of the statement of comprehensive income:*
  - The revenue, expenses and pre-tax profit or loss and the income tax expense of the discontinued operation;

- The gain or loss on disposal of the subsidiary;
- The net cash flows attributable to the operating, investing and financing activities of the subsidiary (IFRS 5.33(b)).

- *Additional disclosures in the notes for assets that have been sold in the current period*

  - A description of the non-current asset;
  - A description of the facts and circumstances of the sale;
  - The gain or loss recognised and, if not separately presented on the face of the statement of comprehensive income, the caption in the statement of comprehensive income that includes that gain or loss (IFRS 5.41).

(ii) Related party issues

Should there be any intra-group transactions involving Mainpart Limited and Subpart Limited from 1 January–1 July 2x05, these will be cancelled on consolidation. In accordance with IAS 24, disclosure requirements would, however, apply in the financial statements of the *separate/individual* companies, as Mainpart and Subpart were related by virtue of one party exercising control over the other (IAS 24.9).

Transactions in the period after the date of disposal (2 July – 31 December 2x05) will also need to be considered in the context of IAS 24. Mainpart Limited's remaining interest during this period is 10%. As this level of shareholding does not normally constitute a related party relationship, no disclosure requirements arise.

(3) Restructuring

IAS 37 states that a provision should be recognised when:

- An entity has a present obligation (legal or constructive) as a result of a past event;

- It is probable that an outflow of resources will be required to settle the obligation;
- A reliable estimate can be made of the amount of the obligation (IAS 37.14).

A provision for restructuring costs is recognised only when the general recognition criteria, outlined above, are met (IAS 37.71). Clearly, as Mainpart Limited has already begun to implement the restructuring of its gardening division, it has a present obligation to do so, and it is probable that an outflow of resources will be required, which can be reliably estimated.

Thus, the following provision should be made in respect of the restructuring plan for Mainpart Limited's gardening division:

	€'000
Redundancy amounts paid early in 2x06	800
Costs of retraining programme*	100
Enhanced staff pensions	1,526.4
– discounted to present value at the Group's WACC of 12%	
$= €220,000 + (€220,000 \times$ annuity factor for 11 years)	
$= €220,000 + (€220,000 \times 5.938)$	
Lease provision (Note 1)	306.2
Total provision required at 31 December 2x05	2,732.6

*IAS 37 (Appendix C, Example 7) states that no provision should be made for training costs, on the basis that there is no obligation, because no obligating event (i.e. training) has taken place. In the case of Mainpart Limited, however, a provision of €100,000 is appropriate, as this is the extent to which redundancy costs cannot (even with retraining) be avoided.

A provision for future operating losses is not permitted by IAS 37, as they do not meet the definition of a liability, which requires that there is a present obligation arising from past events (IAS 37.63).

Note 1: Lease Provision

This represents an onerous contract in the context of IAS 37.10. Thus, provision should be made for the four remaining annual instalments i.e.

€90,000 × 4 = €360,000. When discounted to present value at 12%, this will amount to €306,180 (i.e. €90,000 × 3.402).

Mainpart Limited is confident that half of this amount can be recouped by sub-letting the premises to another tenant. At this point, however, this is a contingent asset, whose recognition is not permitted (IAS 37.31). Details of this probable inflow of economic benefits should, however, be disclosed by way of note where an inflow of economic benefits is regarded as being probable (IAS 37.34).

Journal adjustment

The journal adjustment required in respect of the restructuring of the gardening division can now be put through as follows:

	DR €'000	CR €'000
Increase in provision for restructuring – SOCI P/L	2,732.6	
Provision for restructuring – SOFP		2,732.6
(Being provision for restructuring of gardening division of Mainpart Limited)		

Disclosure issues:

- On the basis of its materiality, the restructuring provision should be disclosed separately in Mainpart Limited's Statement of comprehensive income (and that of the Group), or in the notes, in accordance with IAS 1.87.

- Disclosures should be provided in accordance with IAS 37.84–37.92.

(4) Disposal of Land

The IASB's Conceptual Framework requires that an entity's financial statements should reflect the substance of a transaction. It is apparent that the land in question has not in substance been disposed of by Rent Part Limited. This conclusion is evidenced by its transfer back to the company on 12 January 2x06. The land should therefore continue to be recognised by Rent

Part Limited as an asset at 31 December 2x05, and the following journal adjustment is required:

	DR €'000	CR €'000
Land	800	
Profit on disposal – SOCI P/L	1,200	
Trade and other receivables		2,000

SOLUTION TO
MILLENNIUM GROUP

(a) Adjustments to draft financial statements

(1) Sale of land

IAS 18 *Revenue* states that goods should be recognised as having been sold when all of the following criteria have been satisfied:

- The seller has transferred to the buyer the significant risks and rewards of ownership;
- The seller retains neither continuing managerial involvement to the degree usually associated with ownership nor effective control over the goods sold;
- The amount of revenue can be measured reliably;
- It is probable that the economic benefits associated with the transaction will flow to the seller;
- The costs incurred or to be incurred in respect of the transaction can be measured reliably (IAS 18.14).

It is questionable whether the sale of the land has satisfied these criteria, as the payment of the consideration may be dependent on planning permission being obtained by the purchaser. On the basis that Millennium Plc continues to have significant exposure to the risks and benefits inherent in the asset, no sale should be recognised and the land should continue to be recorded in the financial statements of Millennium Plc.

The journal required to reverse the sale of the land is outlined in Appendix I below – see J/E (i).

The question also arises as to whether the land should, at 31 December 2x05, be classified as being held for sale. For this treatment to apply, the sale must be highly probable (IFRS 5.7). As this is not the case, the land should not be re-classified in the financial statements at 31 December 2x05.

(2) Purchase of building

In accordance with IAS 16 *Property, Plant and Equipment*, there are a number of points to consider in relation to the purchase of the building on 1 January 2x05:

- The useful life of an asset is defined by IAS 16 in terms of the present owner (i.e. the period over which an asset is expected to be available for use by an entity (IAS 16.6)). Thus, 10 years rather than 50 years is the relevant life in this case.

- Residual value is defined by IAS 16.6 as being based on current prices, thus excluding the effects of future inflation (IAS 16.6).

On this basis, the depreciable amount of the building is €100,000 (i.e. €1.6m − €1.5m), and the useful life of the building is 10 years. Thus the depreciation charge for the year ended 31 December 2x05 is €10,000. See Journal Entry (ii) in Appendix I below.

(3) Sale of subsidiary

- As the operations and cash flows of Leading Edge Limited can be clearly distinguished, it is defined as a component of the Group (IFRS 5, Appendix A).

- A discontinued operation is a component of an entity that either has been disposed of, or is classified as held for sale, and

  - represents a major line of business or geographical area of operations, *or*
  - is part of a single co-ordinated plan to dispose of a separate major line of business or geographical area of operations, *or*
  - is a subsidiary acquired exclusively with a view to resale.

Leading Edge had contributed 50% of the Group's data backup sales, with a turnover of €3 million and operating profit of €1 million for the six months ended 30 June 2x05. The

Millennium Group's turnover and operating profit for the year ended 31 December 2x05 were €16.8 million and €7.6 million respectively. Thus, it can be concluded that Leading Edge is a major line of business within the group, and its disposal is classified as a discontinued operation.

Disclosures required:

(i) On the face of the statement of comprehensive income:
A single amount, being the total of the after tax profit or loss of the discontinued operation, and the after tax gain or loss from disposing of the assets comprising the discontinued operation (IFRS 5.33(a)).

(ii) In the notes or on the face of the statement of comprehensive income:

- The revenue, expenses and pre-tax profit or loss and the income tax expense of the discontinued operation;
- The gain or loss on disposal of the subsidiary;
- The net cash flows attributable to the operating, investing and financing activities of the subsidiary (IFRS 5.33(b)–(c)).

(iii) Additional disclosures in the notes for non-current assets that have been sold in the current period:

- A description of the non-current asset;
- A description of the facts and circumstances of the sale;
- The gain or loss recognised and, if not separately presented on the face of the statement of comprehensive income, the caption in the statement of comprehensive income that includes that gain or loss;
- The segment in which Leading Edge is reported under IFRS 8 *Operating Segments*.

(4) Software costs

(a) External purchase of software
Computer software is generally regarded as an intangible asset (IAS 38.9).

An intangible asset should be recognised if:

(i)   it is probable that the expected future economic benefits that are attributable to the asset will flow to the entity; *and*

(ii)   the cost of the asset can be measured reliably (IAS 38.21).

Intangible assets that are acquired separately are assumed to satisfy the probability requirement in (i) above (IAS 38.25).

- Therefore, €700,000 of the purchased software should be capitalised as an intangible asset, as its cost can be reliably measured and its future economic benefits will flow to Millennium Plc (IAS 38.21).

- The other software (€100,000) is an essential component of Millennium Plc's mainframe computer, and should be treated as part of that tangible asset (IAS 38.4).

- The software should be depreciated using an expected useful life of five years, with the exception of the software for the mainframe computer, which should be depreciated over two years.

- See journal entries in section (iii) of Appendix I below.

(b) Software Development

In order to assess whether an internally generated intangible asset meets the criteria for recognition, IAS 38 requires that an entity should classify the generation of the asset into:

- a research phase, and
- a development phase (IAS 38.52).

Assets arising from the **research** phase of an internal project shall **not** be recognised (IAS 38.54).

An intangible asset arising from the **development** phase of an internal project shall be recognised if an entity can demonstrate all of the following (IAS 38.57):

- technical feasibility

- intention to complete the intangible asset and use or sell it

- how the intangible asset will generate probable future economic benefits

- the availability of adequate resources to complete the development

- its ability to measure reliably the expenditure attributable to the intangible asset during its development.

On the basis that these prerequisite conditions are complied with, the expenditure of €500,000, relating to the employment of additional programmers, should be recognised as an intangible asset.

(c) Software acquired for development work

Software costing €400,000 was acquired to assist in the development of a new product costing system, which is currently at the development phase. On the assumption that it satisfies the six criteria in paragraph IAS 38.57, the software costs should be recognised as an intangible asset.

IAS 38 requires that amortisation of intangible assets should commence when the asset is available for use, and that the asset should then be amortised over its useful life (IAS 38.97). See journal entry (iv) in Appendix I below.

(5) Investment in Future Developments Limited

(i) Classification

IFRS 11 *Joint Arrangements* defines a joint venture as a joint arrangement whereby the parties that have joint control of the arrangement have rights to the net assets of the arrangement (IFRS 11.16).

The purchase of the 50% stake in Future Developments Limited appears to satisfy the definition of a joint venture in IFRS 11.

IFRS 11 requires that a joint venturer shall recognise its interest in a joint venture using the equity method (IFRS 11.24).

(ii) Sale of land block by Future Developments Limited to Millennium Plc

When a joint venturer purchases an asset from a joint venture, the joint venturer shall not recognise its share of the profits of the joint venture from the transaction until it re-sells the asset to an independent party.

The profit on sale of the land by Future Developments Limited should therefore be eliminated to the extent of the joint venturer's share in that company (IAS 31.49). Thus, €150,000 (i.e. €300,000 × 50%) of the profit on sale should be eliminated in preparing the consolidated financial statements of the Millennium Group. See journal entry (v) in Appendix I below for details of this adjustment.

Future Developments Limited and Millennium Plc are defined as related parties (IAS 24.9(c)). Thus, subject to its materiality, details of the sale should be disclosed as follows:

- In the group financial statements;
- In the individual/separate financial statements of Future Developments Limited and Millenium Plc.

The disclosures should outline:
- Nature of relationship between Future Developments and Millennium;
- The amounts involved in the transaction;
- Amounts of any outstanding balances (IAS 24.17).

(iii) Sale of inventory by a subsidiary of the group to Future Developments Limited

- IFRS 11 requires that the joint venturer shall recognise only that portion of the gain or loss that is attributable to the interests of the other joint venturers.

- Thus, an adjustment should be made in the Group financial statements eliminating half of the profit of €250,000.

	DR €'000	CR €'000
Cost of sales – SOCI P/L	125	
Investment in Joint Venture		125

(Being adjustment in the Group a/c's on an **equity basis**)

- There are also implications for related party disclosures in accordance with IAS 24:

Subject to its materiality, disclosure of the transaction will be required in the Group financial statements, as the transaction has taken place between a subsidiary of the Group (Century Limited) and a joint venture of the Group (Future Developments Limited).

(iv) **Consolidation adjustment in respect of Joint Venture**
As the JV is included in the Group financial statements on an *equity basis,* it will be necessary to include a consolidation adjustment in respect of the investing group's share of the post-acquisition retained profit of Future Developments Limited. See journal entry (v) in Appendix I below.

Appendix I

(b) Journal Entries in Group Financial Statements

	DR €'000	CR €'000
(i) Reversal of sale of land:		
Land	1,200	
Profit on disposal – SOCI P/L	300	
Trade and other receivables		1,500
(Being cancellation of sale of land)		
Retained earnings – SOFP	200	
Revaluation surplus – SOFP		200
(Being reversal of transfer of revaluation surplus to realised reserves)		
(ii) Depreciation of building		
Depreciation charge – SOCI P/L	10	
Accumulated depreciation		10
(Being depreciation on building for 20x5)		

(iii) Externally purchased software

Equipment	100	
Intangible assets		100

(Being re-classification of software as property, plant and equipment)

Amortisation of intangible assets

Amortisation – SOCI P/L	140	
Intangible asset		140

(Being amortisation of software for 20x5: €700k/5)

Depreciation expense – SOCI P/L	50	
Accumulated depreciation		50

(Being depr. charge on software acquired for mainframe computer for 20x5: €100k/2)

(iv) Software acquired for development work

Development costs	400	
R&D costs – SOCI P/L		400

(Being capitalisation of software costs incurred as part of development work)

(v) Investment in Future Developments Ltd:

- **Sale of land to Millennium Plc**

Share of profit of joint venture – SOCI P/L	150	
Investment in joint venture		150

(Being cancellation of Millennium's share of profit on inter-company sale of land by JV)

- **Consolidation adjustment**

Investment in Future Developments Ltd	407	
Consolidated Retained Earnings		407

(Being investing group's share of post-acq. retained profit of joint venture: i.e. (€4,347,000* − €3,533,000) × 50%)

*As per statement of financial position of Future Developments Limited at 31 December 2x05.

SOLUTION TO
NORMAN EPSTOW LIMITED

(a) Adjustments to draft financial statements

(i) *Termination of toy soldier item sales*

Appendix A of IFRS 5 *Non-current assets held for sale and discontinued operations* defines a component of an entity as ...*operations and cash flows that can be clearly distinguished, operationally and for financial reporting purposes, from the rest of the entity.*

Toy soldier item sales would constitute a component under this definition. For a component to be classified as a discontinued operation, it must be held for sale, or already disposed of, and meet one of the following criteria:

- Represent a major line of business or geographical area of operations;
- Be part of a single co-ordinated plan to dispose of a separate major line of business or geographical area of operations;
- Be a subsidiary acquired exclusively with a view to resale (IFRS 5.32).

Because the toy soldier item sales are part of a larger product group (in 2x05 they comprised approximately 13% of total item sales and 2.6% of total sales) they fail to meet the qualifying conditions in paragraph 32 of the standard, and would not therefore be regarded as a discontinued operation.

To the extent that assets at 31 December 2x05 of the toy soldier item category are retained, it is likely that these assets are required to fill occasional orders from important customers. As such assets are not available for immediate sale, they do not qualify as assets held for sale (IFRS 5.7)

(ii)   *Research and development*
IAS 38 requires that an intangible asset arising from development shall be recognised if six prerequisite criteria are satisfied (IAS 38.57).

The research into developing an alternative to the existing lead-based compound has had positive results. It is probable that Norman Epstow Limited will soon have a substantially improved process for the manufacture of kit sales products. On the assumption that the expenditure satisfies the criteria referred to above, the following accounting treatment will be appropriate:

- IAS 38 states that expenditure on an intangible item that was initially recognised as an expense shall not be recognised as part of the cost of an intangible asset at a later date (IAS 38.71). Thus, it is not permissible to write back the R&D expenditure incurred in 2x04, even though the project now appears to be commercially viable. The write back in the 2x05 Financial Statements will therefore need to be reversed.

  – See journal entry (i) in Appendix I below.

- It seems reasonable that the expenditure in 2x05 should be treated as development costs. It is therefore correct that no charge should be made in the Statement of Comprehensive Income. It will be necessary, however, to reclassify as development costs the €70,000 currently included under trade and other receivables.

  – See journal entry (i) in Appendix I below.

- In accordance with IAS 16 *Property, Plant and Equipment,* it will be necessary to provide for depreciation on the machine purchased in February 2x05. As the machine is being used for development work, however, its future economic benefits are being absorbed by a research project that qualifies as an intangible asset. The depreciation on the machine should therefore be included in development costs as an asset, rather than being charged to profit or loss (IAS 16.49).

  – See journal entry (i) in Appendix I below.

(iii) *Sale of production rights*

The purchase of production rights in relation to miniature figures associated with the Muhammad Ali film can be regarded as the acquisition of an intangible asset. IAS 38 requires that an intangible asset should be derecognised on disposal, and that the gain or loss should be determined as the difference between the net disposal proceeds and the carrying amount of the asset (IAS 38.112–113).

IAS 38 also states that the gain/loss should be recognised in profit or loss, but should not be classified as revenue (IAS 38.113).

Subject to materiality, the profit on disposal should be separately disclosed in the Statement of Comprehensive Income or in the notes, in accordance with IAS 1.97.

– See journal entry (ii) in Appendix I below.

(iv) *Sale of premises*

The disposal proceeds of the premises should be reduced by a provision for repairs. This relates to a condition of sale that the purchaser be compensated for dry rot repairs. Thus, a present obligation exists as a result of a past event, and a provision is required at 31 December 2x05 (IAS 37.14).

A settlement of €20,000 was agreed in February 2x06, which constitutes an adjusting event after the reporting period (IAS 10.9(a)). This should be provided for at 31 December 20x5 (IAS 10.8).

Consideration should also be given to the separate disclosure of the profit on disposal, either in the Statement of Comprehensive Income or in the notes (IAS 1.97).

It will also be appropriate to transfer the unrealised surplus on revaluation of the premises of €84,800 to realised reserves.

Details relating to the purchase and disposal of the premises are outlined below, and the adjustment to the 2x05 financial statements is provided as journal entry (iii) in Appendix I.

	DR €'000	CR €'000
Buildings	120	
Bank		120
(Being purchase of building in 2x02)		

Depreciation expense – SOCI P/L	2.4	
Accumulated depreciation		2.4
(Being depreciation charge for 2x02)		
Depreciation expense – SOCI P/L	2.4	
Accumulated depreciation		2.4
(Being depreciation charge for 2x03)		
Accumulated depreciation	4.8	
Buildings		4.8
(Being offset of accumulated depr. on reval. of bldg at 31 December 2x03)		
Buildings	84.8	
Revaluation surplus – SOCI OCI		84.8
(Being revaluation of building to €200k at 31 Dec. 2x03)		
Depreciation expense – SOCI P/L	4.2	
Accumulated depreciation		4.2
(Being depreciation charge for 2x04: 200k/48)		

Bank	300	
Accumulated depreciation	4.2	
Building		200
Provision for repairs – SOFP		20
Profit on disposal – SOCI P/L		84.2
(Being disposal of building in 2x05)		
Revaluation surplus – SOFP	84.8	
Retained earnings – SOFP		84.8
(Being transfer of unrealised surplus to realised reserves)		

(v) *Joint venture arrangement with Checkmate Limited*
This is a joint operation, which involves the use of the assets and other resources of Norman Epstow and Checkmate, rather than the

establishment of another entity that is separate from the joint operators themselves.

IFRS 11 states that in respect of its interests in a joint operation, a joint operator shall recognise in its financial statements (IFRS 11.20):

- its assets, including its share of any assets held jointly;

- its liabilities, including its share of any liabilities incurred jointly;

- its revenue from the sale of its share of the output arising from the joint operation;

- its share of the revenue from the sale of the output by the joint operation; and

- its expenses, including its share of any expenses incurred jointly.

Thus, the following accounting treatment will apply in relation to Norman Epstow's financial statements:

- the machinery purchased in connection with the manufacture of the chess sets should be included as an asset;

- manufacturing and selling costs of €250,000 should be included in cost of sales;

- cash sales of €360,000 should be recognised as revenue (i.e. 60% of total cash sales);

- inventories of €100,000 should be included as an asset at 31 December 2x05. This is appropriate, as all of the manufacturing costs have been incurred by Norman Epstow;

- IAS 2 requires that inventory be valued at the lower of cost and net realisable value (IAS 2.29). Cost in this case amounts to €100,000 and NRV can be estimated at €377,000 (Note 1). Thus, the closing inventory of chess sets should be included in Norman Epstow's statement of financial position at its cost to date of €100,000.

Note 1 – NRV

	€	
Estimated selling price	480,000*	(assuming a mark up of 300% on manufacturing costs, as earned on chess sets already sold, and adjusted for Norman Epstow's share of revenue)
Less completion costs	(100,000)	
Less selling costs	(3,000)	
NRV	377,000	

– See journal entry (iv) in Appendix I below

*Estimated selling price

	€
Cost of inventory when completed	200,000
Add profit margin @ 300%	600,000
Selling price	800,000
Norman Epstow's share @ 60%	480,000

(vi) *Jointly owned property*

This property is a joint operation, as defined by IFRS 11 *Joint Arrangements.*

The property jointly owned by Norman Epstow is investment property, and should be classified as such, rather than being included under property, plant and equipment.

IAS 40 *Investment Property* permits entities to choose either a fair value model or a cost model for all of its investment properties (IAS 40.30). On the assumption that Norman Epstow Limited opts for the fair value model, its share of the gain arising during the 6 months ended 31 December 2x05 should be included in profit or loss for that period.

Also, Norman Epstow's share of rental income should be included in profit or loss.

See journal entry (v) in Appendix I below.

Appendix I

Journal Entries

	DR €'000	CR €'000
(i) R&D		
Net operating expenses – SOCI P/L	50	
Trade and other receivables		50
(Being reversal of reinstatement of 2x04 development costs)		
Development costs – SOFP	70	
Trade and other receivables		70
(Being reclassification of 2x05 development expenditure)		
Development costs – SOFP	6	
Accumulated depreciation		6
(Being depreciation for 2x05 on machine acquired for development work)		
(ii) Sale of production rights		
Revenue	550	
Intangible assets		250
Profit on disposal of intangible asset – SOCI P/L		300
(Being disposal of production rights)		
(iii) Disposal of premises		
Bank	300	
Accumulated depreciation	4.2	
Building		200
Liability for repair costs – SOFP		20
Profit on disposal of premises – SOCI P/L		84.2
(Being disposal of building in 2x05)		
Revaluation surplus – SOFP	84.8	
Retained earnings – SOFP		84.8
(Being transfer of unrealised surplus to realised reserves)		

(iv) Joint operation – manufacture of chess sets

Machinery	200	
Bank		200
(Being purchase of machinery)		
Cost of sales	40	
Accumulated depreciation machinery		40
(Being depreciation of machinery for 2x05)		
Cost of sales	210	
Bank		210
(Being cost of sales – excluding depreciation)		
Bank	360	
Revenue		360
(Being Norman Epstow's agreed share of revenue)		
Inventory	100	
Cost of sales		100
(Being partly completed chess sets @ 31 December 2x05, valued at cost)		

(v) Joint operation – investment property

Investment property	350	
Property, plant and equipment		350
(Being reclassification of property as an investment property)		
Investment property	100	
Gain on revaluation – SOCI P/L		100
(Being Norman Epstow's share of gain on revaluation of investment property)		
Bank	10	
Rental income – SOCI P/L		10
(Being Norman Epstow's share of rental income)		

SOLUTION TO RIGHT TYPE GROUP

Dartry Maunsell & Co.

Memorandum

To: Martina O'Sullivan

From: A. Senior

Date: 24 February 2x06

Re: Right Type Group

Further to our recent meeting I have now had the opportunity to review the issues arising in respect of the audit of the Right Type Group for the year ended 31 December 2x05. I will deal with each issue in turn.

(1) Establishment of Side Type Limited

IFRS 11 *Joint Arrangements* defines a joint venture as a joint arrangement whereby the parties have rights to the net assets of the arrangement (IFRS 11 Appendix A).

The establishment of Side Type Limited qualifies as a joint venture. IFRS 11 requires that a joint venturer shall recognise its interest in a joint venture using the equity method (IFRS 11.24).

Equity method
Under the equity method, the investment is initially recognised at cost and adjusted thereafter for the post-acquisition change in the investor's share of net assets of the investee. The profit or loss of the investor includes the investor's share of the profit or loss of the investee (IAS 28.3).

The following journal entries will apply in the Group Financial Statements, under the equity method:

	DR €'000	CR €'000
Investment in joint venture	1,500	
Bank		1,500

(Being Right Type's share of cost of setting up Side Type Limited)

	DR €'000	CR €'000
Expenses – SOCI P/L	750	
Bank		750

(Being fee paid by Right Type to Milton Property Care for 9 months ended 31 December 2x05)

	DR €'000	CR €'000
Investment in joint venture	150	
Share of profit – Consolidated SOCI P/L		150

(Being share of profit of Side Type Limited for 9 months ended 31 December 2x05)

Disclosure Issues

Right Type Limited is classified as a related party of Side Type Limited, on the basis that it has joint control over it (IAS 24.9). Subject to materiality, details of transactions between the companies will need to be disclosed as follows:

- In the individual financial statements of Side Type Limited, details of transactions with Right Type;
- Disclosure will be required in the individual financial statements of Right Type Limited of transactions with Side Type Limited;
- Transactions between Right Type and Side Type will also require disclosure in the financial statements of the Right Type Group.

(2) Intangible Assets

(a) *Right Type brand name*
IAS 38 states that *Internally generated brands, mastheads, publishing titles, customer lists and items similar in substance shall not be recognised as intangible assets* (IAS 38.63).

Thus, the sums expended by the Right Type Group in promoting the quality of its brand name should not have been capitalised, but should have been expensed to profit or loss as they were incurred. This constitutes a material prior period error, and it should be corrected retrospectively in the first set of financial statements authorised for issue after its discovery (IAS 8.42).

The Right Type Group's Statement of Changes in Equity will be required to adjust the opening balance of each affected component of equity (i.e. retained earnings), and comparative amounts presented in the financial statements should be adjusted.

Extract from Statement of Changes in Equity for the year ended 31 December 2x05

	Share Capital	Retained Earnings	Total
Balance at 31 December 2x03 as re-stated	X	Y*	X + Y
Profit for the year ended 31 December 2x04 as re-stated	_____	(€0.24m)	(€0.24m)
Restated balance at 1 January 2x05			X + Y − €0.24m
Changes in equity for 2x05	_____	_____	_____
Balance at 31 December 2x05	_____	_____	_____

*Original balance less €1.2m

$[1 \cdot 2 \times \cdot 2]$

The following journal entries will be required:

	DR €'000	CR €'000
Retained earnings	1,440	
Intangible asset		1,440

(Being write-off of Right Type brand up to 31 December 2x04)

Expenses – SOCI P/L	288	
Intangible asset		288

(Being write-off of expenditure on Right Type brand capitalised in year ending 31 December 2x05)

1·2   03
·24   04
———
1·44

1·728
(1·44)
———
·288   05

IAS 8 requires the following disclosure in respect of prior period errors:

- the nature of the prior period error;
- for each prior period presented, to the extent practicable, the amount of the correction;
- the amount of the correction at the beginning of the earliest prior period presented;
- if retrospective restatement is impracticable for a particular prior period, the circumstances that led to the existence of that condition and a description of how and from when the error has been corrected (IAS 8.49).

Additionally, IAS 1 requires that a statement of financial position be presented at the beginning of the earliest comparative period (i.e. 1 January 2x04) when an entity makes a retrospective restatement of items in its financial statements (IAS 1.10(f)).

(b)   Well Build brand

Recognition

IAS 38 states that an intangible asset shall be recognised if:

(i)   it is probable that the expected future economic benefits that are attributable to the asset will flow to the entity; *and*

(ii) the cost of the asset can be measured reliably (IAS 38.21).

IAS 38.25 states that intangible assets which are separately acquired are always considered to satisfy the probability recognition criterion in (i) above. Clearly, the acquisition cost of the Well Build brand can also be measured reliably. Therefore, in accordance with IAS 38, the Well Build brand should be recognised as an intangible asset.

IAS 38 also requires that an intangible asset should be measured initially at its cost (IAS 38.24). It is thus necessary to eliminate the premium above cost attributed to the Well Build brand. The following journal entry will be required:

	DR €'000	CR €'000
Gain on a bargain purchase – SOFP*	1,000	
Intangible assets – Well Build brand		1,000

(Being re-statement of Well Build brand to cost price)

*It was incorrect, in any event, to record this gain in the SOFP. IFRS 3 requires that a gain on a bargain purchase (i.e. negative goodwill) should be recorded in profit or loss by the acquirer (IFRS 3.34).

Measurement after recognition

IAS 38 requires that an entity should choose either the cost model or the revaluation model as its accounting policy, with a similar policy being applied to all assets in the same class (IAS 38.72).

Fair value, for the purposes of revaluations under IAS 38, should be determined by reference to an active market (IAS 38.75). However IAS 38 states that an active market cannot exist for brands, on the basis that each such asset is unique (IAS 38.78).

Thus, it would not be appropriate to revalue the Well Build brand, as clearly there is no active market for this type of asset.

Amortisation

IAS 38 states that, where intangible assets are regarded as having indefinite useful lives, they should not be amortised (IAS 38.107). The decision of the Right Type Group not to amortise the Well Build brand is therefore in accordance with the standard.

In accordance with IAS 36 *Impairment of Assets,* however, an entity is required to test an intangible asset with an indefinite life for impairment, by comparing its recoverable amount with its carrying amount:

- Annually, *and*
- Whenever there is an indication that the intangible asset may be impaired (IAS 36.9–36.10).

Disclosure

The following disclosures are required by IAS 38 for each class of intangible assets:

- Whether the useful lives are indefinite or finite and, if finite, the useful lives or the amortisation rates used;
- The amortisation methods used for intangible assets with finite useful lives;
- The gross carrying amount and any accumulated amortisation at the beginning and end of the period;
- The line item(s) of the statement of comprehensive income in which any amortisation of intangible assets is included;
- A reconciliation of the carrying amount at the beginning and end of the period (IAS 38.118).

(3) Expenditure on assets

(i) *Replacement of lift*

IAS 16 states that parts of property, plant and equipment requiring replacement should be included as part of the cost of the related asset if the expenditure satisfies the recognition criteria in paragraph 7 of the standard (IAS 16.13).

IAS 16.7 states that an asset should be recognised if:

- it is probable that future economic benefits associated with the item will flow to the entity, and
- the cost of the item can be measured reliably.

These prerequisites appear to be satisfied in this case, and the replacement lift will therefore be classified as capital expenditure. The lift should be included as part of the head office building.

IAS 16 requires that each part of an item of property, plant and equipment with a cost that is significant in relation to the total cost of the item shall be depreciated separately (IAS 16.43). Thus, unlike the Group's buildings, which are depreciated over 50 years, the lift should be depreciated over its useful life of 10 years.

In computing the depreciable amount of the lift, the asset's estimated residual value should be deducted from its cost. The residual value should be calculated based on current prices, and not on those expected to prevail in 10 years' time (IAS 16.6).

IAS 16 requires that the carrying amount of those parts that are replaced is derecognised, with the gain or loss being included in profit or loss. Gains should not be classified as revenue (IAS 16.13 & IAS 16.68).

IAS 16 also states that the initial estimate of the costs of dismantling and removing an asset be included in the asset's cost (IAS 16.16). Thus, a corresponding asset will be set up on the basis that the expenditure provides access to future economic benefits. Thus, the estimated present value of the decommissioning expenses (i.e. €30,000) will be provided for and included as part of the cost of the lift. As the decommissioning costs will be a year closer (at 31 December 2x05) to being paid, it will be necessary to unwind the discount by one year during 2x05.

The following journal entries will be required:

	DR €'000	CR €'000
Land & buildings	30	
Provision for decommissioning – SOFP		30
(Being provision for costs of decommissioning the lift)		
Depreciation expense – SOCI P/L	31	
Accumulated depreciation land & buildings		31

(Being depreciation charge on lift for 2x05, based on a depreciable amount of €310,000*, and an estimated useful life of 10 years)

*Cost + decommissioning provision − residual value
  i.e. €300,000 + €30,000 − €20,000

	DR	CR
Finance costs – SOCI P/L	3	
Provision for decommissioning costs – SOFP		3

(Being unwinding of discount during 2x05 @ 10%. Cost in 10 years from 1/1/2x05 = 30k ÷ .386** = €77,720. PV cost at 31/12/2x05 = €77,720 × .424*** = €32,953. Therefore, during 2x05, the discount unwinds by €3,000 (i.e. 32,953 − 30,000).)

 ** .386 = PV factor for year 10 @ 10%
*** .424 = PV factor for year 9 @ 10%

Or simply 30k × 10%

(ii)   *Compliance with fire regulations*

Certain items of property, plant and equipment may be necessary for an entity to obtain the future economic benefits from its other assets. Such items qualify for recognition as assets (IAS 16.11). Fire safety equipment is an example of this type of asset, and capital expenditure on such an asset should be capitalised.

IAS 16 also states that the costs of day-to-day servicing of an asset should be recognised in profit or loss as incurred. The purpose of these expenditures is often described as being for the repair and maintenance of the item of property, plant and equipment (IAS 16.12).

On the basis of the above requirements of IAS 16, the following treatment is recommended in respect of expenditure incurred in connection with fire regulation compliance:

- The repair of fire doors is part of the repair and maintenance of the company's buildings, and this expenditure should be expensed in profit or loss;
- The installation of fire escapes appears to satisfy the requirements of paragraph 11 of IAS 16, and this expenditure should be capitalised as part of land & buildings;
- The purchase of fire safety equipment similarly represents capital expenditure, and this amount should be capitalised as part of fixtures and fittings.

The following journal entries will be required:

	DR €'000	CR €'000
Repairs and maintenance – SOCI P/L	50	
Fixtures and fittings		50
(Being re-classification of fire door repairs as revenue expenditure)		
Accumulated depreciation fixtures & fittings	40	
Depreciation expense – SOCI P/L		40
(Being reversal of original depreciation charge)		

Depreciation expense – SOCI P/L	5	
Accumulated depreciation		
land & buildings		5
(Being depreciation on fire escapes		
for 2x05, on the basis that a full year's		
depreciation @ 2% p.a.		
SL is charged in the year of purchase)		

Depreciation expense – SOCI P/L	10	
Accumulated depreciation		10
fixtures & fittings		
(Being depreciation on safety		
equipment for 2x05, on the basis that		
a full year's depreciation @ 10% p.a.		
RB is charged in the year of purchase)		

(4) Revenue Issues

(i) *Sale of residential homes*

In respect of the completed sales of 12 houses, these should be recorded as revenue in accordance with IAS 18.14:

	DR €'000	CR €'000
Bank/Trade receivables	3,600	
Revenue		3,600
(Being the sale of 12 houses)		
Cost of sales	2,040	
Inventory (SOFP)		2,040
(Being cost of 12 houses)		

A deposit has been received on a further four houses, the sale being dependent on an engineer's report, and on the purchaser being able to raise finance. For revenue to be recorded, the seller must have transferred to the buyer the significant risks and rewards of ownership (IAS 18.14). This does not appear to have happened in this case, and therefore no sale should be recognised by the Right Type Group. The deposits received should be recorded as a liability.

	DR €'000	CR €'000
Bank	80	
Trade and other payables		80

In respect of the remaining eight houses in the development, the lease agreements which have been signed constitute operating leases, as defined by IAS 17.4. These will be recorded as income, on a straight line basis over the lease term (IAS 17.50).

Two of the lessees have, however, signed unconditional contracts to purchase a house, with the December lease instalment being offset against the purchase price. The following journal entries will be required:

	DR €'000	CR €'000
Bank	24	
Lease income – SOCI P/L		24
(Being instalments received on operating leases)		
Lease income – SOCI P/L	2	
Revenue		2
(Being lease instalments offset against buyers' purchase price of houses)		

The signing of unconditional purchase contracts by two customers on the 2 December means that the criteria of IAS 18.14 regarding the sale of goods have been complied with. The following journal entry will be required at 31 December 2x05:

	DR €'000	CR €'000
Trade receivables	598	
Revenue		598
(Being the sale of two houses, net of offsetting lease instalments)		
Cost of sales	340	
Inventory (SOFP)		340
(Being the cost of two houses)		

(ii)   *Provision of security service*

This constitutes the rendering of a service, as outlined in IAS 18 *Revenue*. As the requirements of IAS 18.20 appear to have been met, revenue should be recorded on a percentage of completion basis (IAS 18.21).

As the result of a security breach in November 2x05, however, Property Sites Limited is entitled to a partial refund/reduction of amounts paid/payable. In accordance with IAS 37.14, this represents a present obligation as the result of a past event, and a provision should be recorded at 31 December 2x05.

The following entries are required:

	DR	CR
	€	€
Bank	2,400	
Income from security service – SOCI P/L		2,400

(Being income from security contract for Oct and Nov 2x05)

	DR	CR
Income from security service – SOCI P/L	600	
Provision for customer refund – SOFP		600

(Being provision for refund of November security fee of €1,200 less rental income of €600 for December 2x05)

(5) Land

The land acquired for building purposes would be more in the nature of inventory, were the company to proceed with its diversification plans. As such it should be valued at the lower of cost and net realisable value (IAS 2.28).

The land bank was acquired for a cost of €1 million, and there is a possibility of planning permission being withdrawn, in which case the net realisable value of the land would be €400,000.

Thus, the land should be restated to its cost figure of €1 million. The possible withdrawal of planning permission is akin to a contingent liability, as defined in IAS 37.10. Details should be disclosed in the Financial Statements (IAS 37.28).

The following journal adjustment will be required at 31 December 2x05:

	DR €'000	CR €'000
Revaluation surplus – SOCI OCI	500	
Inventory (i.e. land bank) – SOFP	1,000	
Land		1,500

(Being reclassification of land as a current asset)

The land should also be reclassified as inventory in the financial statements of previous years.

(6) Village Living Concept

This project would appear to satisfy the criteria of IAS 38, *Intangible Assets*, to be classified as development phase research expenditure (IAS 38.57). This was clarified by the success of the rights issue in January 2x06 which provides funding for the completion of the project.

The mobile information office was acquired through a finance lease (as defined in IAS 17.4) and it should be included in property, plant and equipment, with the corresponding leasing liability also being shown in the Financial Statements. The mobile information office should be capitalised at its fair value (€600,000) or, if lower, at the present value of the minimum lease payments (€600,000), each determined at the inception of the lease (IAS 17.20).

IAS 17 requires that the finance charge in a finance lease should be allocated to each period during the lease term so as to produce a constant periodic rate of interest on the remaining balance of the liability (IAS 17.25). A lessee may however use some form of approximation to simplify the calculation (IAS 17.26). The sum of the digits method is employed in this regard, in order to allocate the finance charge relating to the lease of the mobile information office.

In respect of the depreciation of the mobile information office, the annual charge constitutes part of the development cost, and it should be included in the carrying value of that asset (IAS 16.49).

The rights issue is a non-adjusting event after the reporting period (IAS 10.3). As such it should be disclosed in the Financial Statements.

In order to reflect the above requirements, the following journal adjustments should be made:

		€'000	€'000
(i)	Development costs – SOFP	300	
	Labour costs – SOCI P/L		300
	(Being deferral of labour costs incurred in respect of Village Living concept)		
(ii)	Equipment	600	
	Lease obligation – SOFP		600
	(Being capitalisation of mobile office acquired through finance lease)		
(iii)	Lease obligation	100	
	Lease charges – SOCI P/L		100
	(Being reversal of leasing charge to profit or loss)		
(iv)	Development costs – SOFP	120	
	Accumulated depreciation		120
	(Being depreciation for 2x05 on mobile office)		
(v)	Development costs – SOFP	50	
	Lease obligation – SOFP		50
	(Being leasing interest charge for 2x05 capitalised as part of development costs – see note 1)		

Note 1:

Amortisation of lease interest

The sum of digits method is used to approximate a constant periodic rate of interest on the remaining balance of the liability.

Periods	Interest for period(Rounded)	Relevant period
7	€200,000 × 7/28 = 50,000	6 M/E 31/12/2x05
6	€200,000 × 6/28 = 43,000	6 M/E 30/6/2x06
5	€200,000 × 5/28 = 36,000	6 M/E 31/12/2x06
4	€200,000 × 4/28 = 29,000	6 M/E 30/6/2x07

7 × 4 = 28

4 years 7 periods

3	€200,000 × 3/28 =	21,000	6 M/E 31/12/2x07
2	€200,000 × 2/28 =	14,000	6 M/E 30/06/2x08
1	€200,000 × 1/28 =	7,000	6 M/E 31/12/2x08
–	(Note 2)		
28		200,000	

Note 2:   No interest is allocated to the final period, as the lease instalments are payable in advance. Thus, no capital will be outstanding for the final six months of the lease term.

Note 3:   At 31 December 2x05, the outstanding lease liability in the statement of financial position will be computed as follows:

	€' 000
Current liability (€200k less interest of €93k)	107
Non-current liability (€500k less interest of €107k)	393
	500

Lease interest accrued of €50,000 will also be included in current liabilities.

SOLUTION TO
TRACER GROUP

Clarke, Scriven & Co.

Memorandum

To: **Julie Crimson**

From: **A. Senior**
Date: **24 March 2x06**

Re: **Tracer Group**

Further to our recent meeting I have now had the opportunity to review the issues arising in respect of the audit of the Tracer Group for the year ended 31 December 2x05. I will deal with each issue in turn.

Issue (a) – Construction of Head Office Building

(i) *Initial Cost of Head Office Building*

The head office building was included in the non-current assets of Tracer Limited at 30 September 2x05 at a total cost of €4.17 million.

Property, plant and equipment should initially be measured at cost (IAS 16.15). IAS 16 states that *cost* comprises an asset's purchase price together with any costs directly attributable to bringing the asset into working condition for its intended use.

Directly attributable costs include the following (IAS 16.17):

- costs of site preparation
- professional fees.

The overriding requirement in capitalising directly attributable costs is that they must be *incremental,* and would therefore have been avoided if the asset had not been constructed or acquired.

Costs that are **not** incremental costs of an item of property, plant and equipment include administration and other general overhead costs (IAS 16.19).

Thus, the head office building of Tracer Limited should have been capitalised, exclusive of general administrative overheads of €400,000. Consequently, the following correcting journal entry is required:

	DR €'000	CR €'000
Administrative expenses – SOCI P/L	400	
Property, plant and equipment		400

(ii) Borrowing Costs

Borrowing costs that are directly attributable to the construction of a qualifying asset should be capitalised as part of the cost of that asset (IAS 23.9).

Capitalisation should commence when expenditures are being incurred, borrowing costs are being incurred and activities that are necessary to prepare the asset for its intended use or sale are in progress (IAS 23.17).

Capitalisation should however be suspended during periods in which active development is interrupted (IAS 23.20). In the case of Tracer Limited therefore, no costs should be capitalised that relate to the period of work stoppage, 1 April–30 June 2x05. Capitalisation should cease when substantially all of the activities necessary to prepare the asset for its intended use or sale are complete, which in Tracer Limited's case is 30 September 2x05 (IAS 23.22).

The amount of borrowing costs to be capitalised should therefore be computed as follows:

Item	Cost €'000	Timescale from commencement on 1 January to date of completion on 30 September (excluding work stoppage period of 3 months)	Annual Equivalent €'000
Site clearance	200	6 months	100
Legal fees	70	6 months	35
April Certificate	1,600	3 months	400
Sept. Certificate	1,900	0 months	
Total	3,770		535

To the extent that an entity borrows funds generally and uses them for the purpose of obtaining a qualifying asset, the entity shall determine the amount of borrowing costs eligible for capitalisation by applying a capitalisation rate to the expenditures on the asset (IAS 23.14). The capitalisation rate should be the weighted average of the borrowing costs that are outstanding during the period (IAS 23.14).

The interest rate was 8% from 1 January – 31 March, and 9% from 1 July to 30 September. Therefore, the weighted average rate for the relevant period under review (excluding 3 months' work stoppage) was 8.5%.

When this is applied to the relevant annualised costs of €535,000, the borrowing costs to be capitalised amount to €45,475. The following journal entry is therefore required:

	DR €'000	CR €'000
Property, plant & equipment	45.5	
Bank		45.5

(iii) Depreciation

Depreciation begins when an asset is available for use (IAS 16.55) which, in the case of the new head office building, is the 30 September. Three months' depreciation is therefore charged as follows:

	DR €'000	CR €'000
Depreciation expense – SOCI P/L	19.1	
Accumulated depreciation		19.1

(Being depreciation on head office building as follows: ((€4.17m – €400k + €45.5k) × 2% × 3/12)

(iv) *Revaluation at 31 December 2x05*

It is normal practice that accumulated depreciation on build-ings is offset against the gross carrying value when property assets are being revalued (IAS 16.35). The following entry will therefore be required at 31 December 2x05, to revalue the head office building to €6 million:

	DR €'000	CR €'000
Accumulated depreciation	19.1	
Property, plant & equipment		19.1
Property, plant & equipment	2,203.6	
Revaluation surplus – SOCI OCI		2,203.6

(Being revaluation of building at 31 December 2x05:
€6m –(€3.77m + €45.5k – €19.1k))

Revaluation surplus – SOCI OCI	446	
Deferred tax provision – SOFP		446

(Being deferred tax on revaluation surplus @ 20%)*

*Deferred tax is levied on the amount by which the asset is revalued in excess of its original cost. Borrowing costs are excluded from cost for this purpose, as it is assumed that they will not be deductible in computing the chargeable gain. Therefore, the amount of deferred tax is computed as: (€6m – €3.77m) × 20%.

(v) *Accounting Policy Note*

Borrowing costs incurred in respect of the construction of qualifying assets are treated as part of the cost of those assets. Capitalisation commences when expenditures are being incurred, borrowing costs are being incurred, and activities that are necessary to prepare the asset for its intended use are in progress. Capitalisation of borrowing costs is suspended during extended periods in which active development is interrupted.

Issue (b) – Government Grant

Government grants should be recognised when there is reasonable assurance that:

- an entity will comply with any conditions attached to the grants, *and*
- the grants will be received (IAS 20.7).

Comps Limited may have been incorrect in recognising the government grant of €100,000, if there was not reasonable assurance of the conditions relating to employment targets being met.

On 31 December 2x05, it will be necessary to provide for the repayment of the grant, following the government inspection in July of that year. This provision is necessary, in accordance with IAS 37, *Provisions, Contingent Liabilities and Contingent Assets,* as there is a 60% probability that the grant will have to be repaid.

IAS 20 states that a government grant which becomes repayable shall be accounted for as a revision to an accounting estimate (IAS 20.32).

Comps Limited has also failed to capitalise the decommissioning costs of the machine, which is a requirement of IAS 16 (IAS 16.16(c)). This does not constitute a material error, however, and retrospective adjustment is not required under IAS 8.

The following correcting journal entries are required:

	DR €'000	CR €'000
Plant and machinery	100	
Provision for grant repayment – SOFP		100
(Being reinstatement of asset to gross cost, and creation of provision for repayment of grant)		
Depreciation expense – SOCI P/L	19	
Accumulated depreciation		19
(Being two years' depreciation originally avoided due to deduction of grant from the asset in 2x04)		

Plant and machinery	10	
Provision for decommissioning – SOFP		10*
(Being provision for decommissioning of machine)		

Depreciation expense – SOCI P/L	1.9	
Accumulated depreciation		1.9
(Being two years' depreciation on capitalised decommissioning costs)		

*This provision has not been discounted to present value on the basis that the effect of the time value of money was not material.

Issue (c) – Share Options

The increase in the rights to an entity's shares requires an increase in a component of equity. When the payment for goods or services does not represent an asset, IFRS 2 *Share Based Payment* requires the offsetting entry to be expensed.

Tracer Limited issued share options on 31 December 2x03 to its key executives, with the exercise of the options conditional on the completion of two years' service from that date. The issue of these options is considered to relate to the services the employees will provide over the vesting period, and therefore the fair value of the share-based payment, determined at the grant date, should be expensed over the two years commencing on the 1 January 2x04.

Each of the options issued to the 10 executives of Tracer Limited has a fair value of €.8 at the 31 December 2x03, the date of grant of the options. On the basis that one executive does not qualify for the options, the total expense is therefore €720,000 (100,000 × 9 × €.8). In accordance with IFRS 2, this should be accounted for as follows:

	DR €'000	CR €'000
Share option expense – SOCI P/L	400	
Equity reserve – SOFP		400

(Being estimated cost of share option scheme for year ended 31 December 2x04, based on the allocation of the fair value at option grant date over the vesting period (10 × 100k × €.8/2) as all 10 executives were expected to qualify as at that date)

Share option expense – SOCI P/L	320	
Equity reserve – SOFP		320

(Being estimated cost of share option scheme for year ended 31 December 2x05, based on the allocation of the fair value at option grant date over the vesting period ((9 × 100k × €.8) − €400k))

Eight executives exercised their options on 31 December 2x05 and they each paid a total of €100,000 for their shares. This should be recorded by Tracer Limited as follows:

	DR €'000	CR €'000
Bank	800	
Equity reserve – SOFP	640	
Ordinary Share Capital		400
Share Premium		1,040

In respect of the remaining executive, a balance of €80,000 will be held in reserves, pending a decision on the exercise rights of Patrick Cudmore, the executive dismissed by Tracer Limited.

Mr Cudmore, who was dismissed in April 2x05, immediately instigated legal proceedings against the company. In February 2x06, when the financial statements were authorised for issue, it was likely that he would be awarded €500,000 in compensation. It was also possible that he would be awarded an additional €400,000.

As there was a present obligation at 31 December 2x05, resulting from a past event, a provision of €500,000 should be recognised in the financial statements (IAS 37.14). There was also a contingent liability of €400,000, and this should be disclosed by way of note (IAS 37.28).

The following journal entry is required in respect of the financial statements of Tracer Limited for the year ended 31 December 2x05:

	DR €'000	CR €'000
Compensation expense – SOCI P/L	500	
Provision for compensation – SOFP		500
(Being provision for compensation award)		

Issue (d) – Disposal of Shares

(i) *Separate financial statements of Tracer Limited*

The profit or loss on disposal will be computed as the difference between the disposal proceeds of the shares and their cost.

	€'000
Disposal proceeds	12,000
Less:	
Cost of shares (€9 million × 6/9)	(6,000)
Profit on disposal	6,000

The following journal entry will be required in the separate financial statements of Tracer Limited in respect of the disposal:

	DR €'000	CR €'000
Bank	12,000	
Investment in Airlight Limited		6,000
Profit on disposal – SOCI P/L		6,000*

*If this is considered a material amount, its separate disclosure is required by IAS 1 *Presentation of Financial Statements,* either on the face of the statement of comprehensive income or in the notes (IAS 1.97).

(ii) *Group Financial statements*

If a parent loses control of a subsidiary, in accordance with IFRS 10, it should:

- derecognise the assets (including any goodwill) and liabilities of the subsidiary at their carrying amounts at the date that control is lost
- derecognise the carrying amount of any non-controlling interests in the former subsidiary at the date when control is lost
- recognise any investment retained in the former subsidiary at its fair value at the date when control is lost
- recognise the fair value of the consideration received
- recognise any resulting difference as a gain or loss in profit or loss attributable to the parent (IFRS 10.98).

From the perspective of the Financial Statements of the Group, the disposal of a controlling interest in Airlight Limited is represented as follows:

	€'000	€'000
Consideration received		12,000
Investment retained at fair value (€10.5m × 30%)		3,150
Non-controlling interests at date of disposal (€10.5m × 10%; based on % of net assets)		1,050
		16,200
Less:		
Assets less liabilities of the subsidiary at their carrying amounts at the date that control is lost*		(10,500)
Goodwill eliminated on disposal/loss of control		(4,500)
Profit on disposal of Airlight Limited – Consolidated SOCI P/L		1,200

*The amount of identifiable net assets at 30 September 2x05 is computed as follows:

Identifiable net assets when 90% stake in Airlight was acquired (i.e. €5m) + Post-acquisition retained earnings of Airlight up to 30 September 2x05 of €5.5m (i.e. (€7m + (€2m × 9/12)) − €3m).

Airlight Limited ceases to be consolidated as a subsidiary of the Tracer Group on 30 September 2x05, and its income and expenses are included in the consolidated financial statements until that date (IFRS 10.20). At that date, by virtue of Tracer Limited being able to exercise significant influence over Airlight Limited, it will become an associate of the Group (IAS 28.2). The remaining investment in Airlight Limited will be carried at its fair value of €3.15m, at the date when control is lost (IFRS 10.25).

The following journal entry will be required in the group financial statements in respect of the disposal, and the recognition of the retained investment in Airlight Limited as an investment in an associate:

	DR €'000	CR €'000
Bank	12,000	
Non-controlling interests	1,050	
Investment in Associate	3,150	

Goodwill	4,500
Identifiable net assets	10,500
Profit on disposal – SOCI P/L	1,200

The results of Airlight, after disposal, will be included in the Group Accounts using equity accounting. Therefore, the following journal entry will be required in the year ended 31 December 2x05:

	DR €'000	CR €'000
Investment in associate	150	
Share of profit of associate – SOCI P/L		150

(Being group share of associate's profit for the three months ended 31 December 2x05: €2m × 30% × 3/12)

(iii) Disclosure requirements relating to the disposal of shares in Airlight Limited
The disposal of the shares in Airlight Limited constitutes a discontinued operation, as defined by IFRS 5. The *group* financial statements should disclose:

(I)   A single amount on the face of the statement of comprehensive income comprising the total of:

    (i) the post-tax profit or loss of discontinued operations, and
    (ii) the post-tax gain or loss on disposal (IFRS 5.33 (a)).

(II) An analysis of the single amount in (a) into:

    (i)   the revenue, expenses and pre-tax profit or loss of discontinued operations
    (ii) the related income tax expense as required by IAS 12
    (iii) the gain or loss on disposal and the related income tax expense as required by IAS 12.

The analysis may be presented in the notes or on the face of the statement of comprehensive income (IFRS 5.33 (b)).

(III) The net cash flows attributable to the operating, investing and financing activities of discontinued operations (IFRS 5.33 (c)).

The Tracer Group will be required to re-present the above disclosures for prior periods presented in the financial statements (IFRS 5.34).

SOLUTION TO
VERSATILE GROUP

Turnbull Bramston & Co.

Memorandum

To: **Frank DeCourcey**

From: **A. Senior**
Date: **24 February 2x06**

Re: **Versatile Group**

Further to our recent meeting I have now had the opportunity to review the issues arising in respect of the audit of the Versatile Group for the year ended 31 December 2x05. I will deal with each issue in turn.

Issue (a) – Disposal of Excess Limited

(i) *Separate financial statements of Versatile Limited*
Excess Limited will have been recorded at cost as a financial asset in the financial statements of Versatile Limited. Subsequent adjustments will have been made only in respect of dividends received/receivable from Excess Limited.

The profit on disposal will be computed as the net disposal proceeds, less the original cost of investment – see the journal entry in (iii) below.

IAS 37 *Provisions, Contingent Liabilities and Contingent Assets,* requires a provision to be recognised when:

- an entity has a present obligation as a result of a past event;
- it is probable that an outflow of resources will be required to settle the obligation; *and*
- a reliable estimate can be made of the amount of the obligation (IAS 37.14).

As a result of the sale of Excess Limited, Versatile has an obligation to repay any unrecorded liabilities to the purchaser. Thus, it will be necessary to provide for unrecorded liabilities of €10 million in respect of the indemnity provided by Versatile Limited.

(ii) *Group financial statements*

In accordance with IFRS 3 *Business Combinations,* goodwill arising on the acquisition of Excess Limited will have been calculated as the future economic benefits arising from assets acquired that are not individually identified and separately recognised (IFRS 3, Appendix A).

IFRS 10 *Consolidated Financial Statements* requires that a subsidiary be consolidated up to the date that a parent ceases to exercise control over it (IFRS 10.20). On the 30 September 2x05, Versatile Limited disposed of its entire shareholding in Excess Limited, and therefore ceased to exercise control over it from that date.

If a parent loses control over a subsidiary, in accordance with IFRS 10, it should (IFRS 10.25):

- derecognise the assets and liabilities of the former subsidiary from the consolidated SOFP
- recognise any investment retained in the former subsidiary at its fair value when control is lost
- recognise the gain or loss associated with the loss of control.

In respect of the disposal of Excess Limited, this is represented as follows:

	€'000
Consideration received	250,000
Non-controlling interests at date of disposal (€115m × 20%)	23,000
	273,000

Less:

Assets less liabilities of the subsidiary at their carrying amounts at the date that control is lost (€40m + (€100m − €25m))	(115,000)	
Unrecorded liabilities	(10,000)	
Goodwill (€62m − (€40m × 80%))	(30,000)	
Profit on disposal of Versatile Limited – Consolidated SOCI P/L	118,000	

The journal entries to effect the above are outlined in (iii) below.

Group revenue will be reduced by €187.5 million (€200 million × 125% × 9/12) in respect of goods sold by Mercer Limited to Excess Limited from 1 January 2x05 to the date of disposal. Group cost of sales will be reduced by an equivalent amount. No adjustment will be required in respect of intra-group profit on inventory, as Excess Limited is no longer a subsidiary of the Group at 31 December 2x05.

See the journal entries in (iii) below.

(iii) Journal entries

	DR €'m	CR €'m
Separate Financial Statements of Versatile Limited:		
Investment in Excess Limited	62	
Bank		62
(Being purchase of shares in Excess Limited several years ago)		
Bank	250	
Investment in Excess Limited – SOCI P/L		62
Indemnity provision – SOFP		10
Profit on disposal of Excess Limited – SOCI P/L		178
(Being profit on disposal of Excess Limited on 30 September 2x05)		
Group Financial Statements		
Identifiable net assets	40	
Goodwill (€62m − (€40m × 80%))	30	
Bank		62
Non-controlling interests – SOFP		8

(Being purchase of shares in Excess Limited several years ago)

Revenue	187.5	
Cost of Sales		187.5

(Being elimination of intra-group sales for
  9 months ended 30 September 2x05
  i.e. €200m × 125% × 9/12)

Net assets	75	
Consolidated retained earnings		60
Non-controlling interests – SOFP		15

(Being post-acquisition retained profit of
  Excess Limited)

Bank	250	
Non-controlling interests – SOFP	23	
Net assets		115
Goodwill		30
Indemnity provision – SOFP		10
Profit on disposal – SOCI P/L		118

(Being disposal of Excess Limited)

(iv) *Disclosure requirements*

In the financial statements of Versatile Limited, the profit on disposal of €178 million will be disclosed separately in the Statement of Comprehensive Income or in the notes, in accordance with IAS 1 *Presentation of Financial Statements* (IAS 1.97). A similar disclosure will be required in the Group Financial Statements in respect of the Group's profit on disposal of €118 million.

The disposal of Excess Limited is a discontinued operation, as defined by IFRS 5 *Non-current assets held for sale and discontinued operations* (IFRS 5, Appendix A). The following disclosures are required:

- The sum of the post-tax profit or loss of the discontinued operation and the post-tax gain on disposal should be presented as a single amount on the face of the Statement of Comprehensive Income (IFRS 5.33(a));
- Detailed disclosure of revenue, expenses, pre-tax profit or loss, and related income taxes is required either in the notes, or on the

face of the Statement of Comprehensive Income in a section distinct from continuing operations (IFRS 5.33 (b));

- The net cash flows attributable to the operating, investing and financing activities of the discontinued operation. These disclosures may be presented either in the notes or on the face of the financial statements (IFRS 5.33 (c)).

IAS 24 *Related Party Disclosures* regards fellow subsidiaries, Mercer and Excess, as being related parties, because they are members of the same group (IAS 24.9). Intra-group sales in the period 1 January 2x05–30 September 2x05 will be cancelled on consolidation, and therefore no disclosure requirement arises in respect of the Group Financial Statements.

Disclosure will be required however in the individual financial statements of Mercer Limited and Excess Limited of sales of €187.5 million by Mercer to Excess arising in the nine months ended 30 September 2x05.

Issue (b) – Revaluation of Land

The accounting treatment of this asset will be determined in accordance with IAS 16 *Property, Plant and Equipment.*

At 31 December 2x04 the land was revalued to €80 million, reflecting its development potential. This treatment was fully in accordance with IAS 16, which permits companies to adopt a revaluation policy, as long as it applies to all assets in the same class (IAS 16.29).

Due to the Council decision not to allow the shopping centre to proceed, the asset suffered an impairment, as there was a reduction in its future economic benefits, and it was reduced to a valuation of €30 million at 31 December 2x05. In accordance with IAS 36 *Impairment of Assets,* this write-down should be offset against a previous surplus on the same asset, any excess being charged to profit or loss (IAS 36.60).

It will be necessary to provide for deferred tax on the remaining revaluation surplus (IAS 12.15). The fact that deferred tax was not provided previously constitutes an error. It is unlikely however to be considered a material error, particularly in view of the fact that the gain on the asset was unrealised and therefore was not recognised in profit or loss. Thus, retrospective restatement is **not** required.

Journal entries

	DR €'m	CR €'m
Land	15	
Bank		15
(Being purchase of land in 2x03)		
Land	65	
Revaluation surplus – SOCI OCI		65
(Being revaluation of land at 31 December 2x04)		
Revaluation surplus – SOCI OCI	50	
Land		50
(Being impairment loss at 31 December 2x05)		
Revaluation surplus – SOCI OCI	3	
Deferred tax provision – SOFP		3
(Being deferred tax on remaining revaluation surplus of €15 million @ CGT rate of 20%)		

Issue (c) – Work in Progress/Development Site

The site acquired by Minstrel Limited would be regarded as a current asset, as it will be used by the company for the construction of retail units, and is therefore akin to inventory. IAS 2 requires that inventories be valued at the lower of cost and net realisable value, and the site should not therefore have been revalued (IAS 2.28). It will be necessary to reverse the revaluation as follows:

	DR €'m	CR €'m
Revaluation surplus – SOCI OCI	15	
Land		15

(Being reversal of previous revaluation)

The following journal entries are required in respect of the 6211Y contract:

	DR €'m	CR €'m
Contract a/c	15.5	
Bank/Trade payables		15.5
(Being production costs to date at 31 December 2x05)		
Cost of sales	12.2	
Contract a/c		12.2
(Being production costs of work certified at 31 December 2x05)		
Contract a/c	15	
Revenue		15
(Being value of work certified at 31 December 2x05)		
Trade receivables	8.8	
Contract a/c		8.8
(Being amounts invoiced on contract for the year ended 31 December 2x05)		
Bank	6.3	
Trade receivables		6.3
(Being amounts received from client)		

Extracts from Financial Statements of Minstrel Limited:

Statement of Comprehensive Income for the year ended 31 December 2x05

	€'m
Revenue	15
Less Cost of Sales	12.2
Gross profit on 6211Y contract	2.8

IAS 11 requires that, when the outcome of a contract can be estimated reliably, contract revenue and contract costs shall be recognised as revenue and expenses, by reference to the stage of completion of the contract activity at the end of the reporting period (IAS 11.22).

The profit recognised on the 6211Y contract at 31 December 2x05 cannot exceed the ultimate profit on the contract. It is necessary therefore to calculate the overall expected outcome of the contract as follows:

	€'m	€'m
Contract price		28.5
Less:		
Costs to date	15.5	
Costs to complete	7.7	
		23.2
Estimated final profit on contract 6211Y		5.3

As the contract is expected to provide an eventual profit of €5.3 million, it is appropriate, on a percentage of completion basis, to recognise profit of €2.8 million (i.e. value of work certified of €15m less cost of work certified of €12.2m) at 31 December 2x05.

Statement of Financial Position of Minstrel Limited at 31 December 2x05

	€'m
Current assets	
Amount recoverable on contracts (note 1)	9.5
Trade and other receivables	2.5

Note 1: Amount recoverable on contracts

Item	6211Y Contract €'m
Costs to date	15.5
Add recognised profits	2.8

	18.3
Less amounts billed	(8.8)
Net Amount	9.5

Issue (d) – Research & Development

(i) Expenditure incurred in connection with 'the wizmo' must satisfy the six prerequisite conditions of IAS 38 *Intangible Assets,* to be classified as development costs (IAS 38.57). On the assumption that it does comply with these criteria, expenditure in relation to 'the wizmo' should be capitalised.

IAS 16 *Property, Plant and Equipment* states that on some occasions the future economic benefits embodied in an asset are absorbed in producing other assets. In this case the depreciation charge constitutes part of the other asset, and is included in its carrying amount (IAS 16.49).

As the machine purchased on 1 January 2x05 is being utilised for the 'wizmo' project, the related depreciation should therefore be capitalised as part of development costs.

(ii) Journal entries

	DR €'m	CR €'m
Development costs – SOFP	6.5	
Bank/Trade and other payables		6.5
(Being the capitalisation of development costs in accordance with IAS 38)		
Machinery	2.5	
Bank/Trade and other payables		2.5
(Being purchase of machine for development)		
Development costs – SOFP	0.5	
Accumulated depreciation		0.5
(Being depreciation for 2x05, capitalised in accordance with IAS 16)		

SOLUTION TO VORSTER GROUP

1. General

(a) *Motor Factors Limited*

A subsidiary is defined by IFRS 10 *Consolidated Financial Statements* as *an entity that is controlled by another entity* (IFRS 10, Appendix A). As Vorster Limited holds a majority (80%) of the voting rights in Motor Factors Limited, the latter company is therefore a subsidiary of Vorster Limited. It should be accounted for using the acquisition method, and the acquisition cost and the assets and liabilities of Motor Factors at acquisition date should be measured at fair value.

As it is impracticable to prepare interim financial statements for Motor Factors up to 31 December 2x05, the financial statements for the year ended 31 October 2x05 may be used for the purpose of preparing consolidated financial statements, as these do not differ by more than three months from those used by the Group (IFRS 10, Appendix B92). The financial statements of Motor Factors should however be adjusted for the effects of significant items or events that occur between the 31 October 2x05 and the 31 December 20x5.

(b) *Auto Parts Limited*

A joint venture is a joint arrangement whereby the parties that have joint control of the arrangement have rights to the net assets (IFRS 11, Appendix A). Auto Parts was set up by Vorster Limited and Magnus Limited to buy scrapped cars and store the parts for sale. Vorster Limited and Magnus Limited exercise joint control over Auto Parts Limited for their mutual benefit.

Thus, Auto Parts is a joint venture and it should be accounted for using the equity method in accordance with IAS *28 Investments in Associates and Joint Ventures*.

(c) *Cycle Accessories Limited*

IFRS 10 *Consolidated Financial Statements* states that consolidation of an investee should cease when the investor loses control of the investee. Vorster Limited sold this subsidiary on 30 September and, in accordance with IFRS 10, it should be included in the group financial statements as a subsidiary until that date.

Cycle Accessories constitutes a discontinued operation under IFRS 5. A single amount (€270,000) is disclosed on the face of the statement of comprehensive income, comprising the total of:

  – the post-tax profit of Cycle Accessories (€188,000), and
  – the post-tax gain on disposal of the disposal group constituting the discontinued operation (€82,000) (IFRS 5.33 (a)).

See Appendix I below.

The results of Cycle Accessories will also be classified as a discontinued operation in the 2x04 Statement of Comprehensive Income.

An analysis of the results of Cycle Accessories is required, either in the notes or on the face of the statement of comprehensive income. If presented on the face of the statement of comprehensive income, it should be presented separately in a section identified as relating to discontinued operations (IFRS 5.33 (b)).

2. Consolidated Statement of Financial Position

Consolidated Statement of Financial Position of the Vorster Group as at 31 December 2x05*

	€'000	€'000
Assets		
Non-current assets		
Freehold land and bldgs @ NBV		1,200
Plant and mach. @ NBV		1,200

Goodwill	647
Investment in joint venture ((780 × 50%) − 30)	360
	3,407
Current assets	
Inventory	1,550
Trade receivables	1,500
Bank	950
	4,000
Total assets	7,407
Equity and liabilities	
Equity attributable to equity-holders	
of the parent	
Ordinary share capital	450
Capital reserves	200
Retained earnings (See D(ii))	3,215
	3,865
Non-controlling interest (See D(i))	207
Total equity	4,072
Non-current liabilities	
Deferred tax	25
Long-term loans	970
	995
Current liabilities	
Trade payables	1,560
Taxation	780
Total current liabilities	2,340
Total equity and liabilities	7,407

* The consolidated statement of financial position contains 100% of the assets and liabilities of Vorster and Motor Factors.

3. **Vorster Group – Consolidated Statement of Comprehensive Income for the year ended 31 December 2x05** (See Appendix I(a) below)

	2x05 €'000	2x04 €'000
Continuing operations		
Revenue	4,000	
Cost of sales	(2,530)	
Gross profit	1,470	
Other income	330	
Distribution costs	(350)	
Administrative expenses	(475)	
Share of profit of joint venture	(210)	
Finance costs	200	
Profit before tax	985	
Income tax expense	(400)	
Profit for the period from continuing operations	585	
Profit for the period from discontinued operations	270	
Profit for the period	855	
Attributable to:		
Owners of the parent	855	

Lecture Note:

Motor Factors was acquired on 31 October 2x05, and has prepared its financial statements for the year ended 31 October 2x05. Thus, as none of its results relate to the post-acquisition period, they are not included in the consolidated statement of comprehensive income for 2x05.

Appendix I – Workings

(a) Consolidated Statement of Comprehensive Income for the year ended 31 December 2x05

	Vorster Limited	Cycle Accessories (9/12)	Total
	€'000	€'000	€'000
Revenue	4,000	750	4,750
Cost of sales	(2,500)	(225)	(2,725)
Adjustment – inventory profit	(30)		(30)
Gross profit	1,470	525	1,995
Other income	330	–	330
Distribution costs	(350)	(90)	(440)
Administrative expenses	(475)*	(60)	(535)
Finance costs	(200)	(75)	(275)
Profit on disposal of Cycle Accessories		82**	82
Share of profit of joint venture	210		210
Profit before tax	985	382	1,367
Income tax expense	(400)	(112)	(512)
Profit for the period	375	270	855
Ret. profit @ 1/1/05	1,755	430	2,185
Ret. profit @ 31/12/05	2,130	700	3,040

*Includes write-off of professional fees relating to the acquisition of Motor Factors Limited.

** Group profit of €82,000 (rounded – see (B) (ii) below), relating to the disposal of Cycle Accessories is shown in that company's column, so as to obtain a single amount of €270,000 as the profit for the period from discontinued operations.

This amount is separately disclosed in the group statement of comprehensive income, as required by IFRS 5.33. It represents the sum of:

– post-tax profit of the discontinued operation of €188,000, and
– post-tax gain of €82,000 recognised on the disposal of the assets constituting the discontinued operation.

(b) Profit on Disposal of Cycle Accessories Limited

(i)   *Separate financial statements of Vorster Limited*
The profit on disposal of Cycle Accessories Limited recognised in the separate financial statements of Vorster Limited is €700,000. This represents the excess of consideration received over the cost of the investment.

(ii)   *Financial statements of the Vorster Group*
When a parent loses control over a subsidiary, in accordance with IFRS 10, it should:

- derecognise the assets and liabilities of the former subsidiary

- recognise any investment retained at its fair value when control is lost

- recognise the gain or loss associated with the loss of control attributable to the former controlling interest (IFRS 10.25).

This is represented as follows:

	€'000
Consideration received	900
Less:	
Assets less liabilities of the subsidiary at their carrying amounts at the date that control is lost (€1,230,000 + (€250,000 × ¾)) — €600,000	817.5
Group Profit on disposal of Cycle Accessories	82.5

(c) Journal Entries

(i) *Relating to the acquisition of Motor Factors*
In accordance with IFRS 3, the following consolidation adjustments are required:

	DR €'000	CR €'000
Acquisition expenses – SOCI P/L Vorster Ltd	25	
Investment in Motor Factor		25
(Being professional fees previously included as cost of investment – now written off to profit or loss)		
Land & buildings	100	
Revaluation surplus – Motor Factors		75
Deferred tax provision – SOFP		25
(Being revaluation of non-current assets of Motor Factors at acquisition date)		
Revaluation surplus – Motor Factors	75	
Cost of control		60
Non-controlling interests		15
(Being allocation of revaluation surplus at acquisition date)		
Cost of control in Motor Factors	144	
Non-controlling interests	36	
Current tax payable		180
(Being accrual for income tax at acquisition date)		
Provision for reorganisation costs – SOFP	90	
Cost of control		72
Non-controlling interests		18

(Being reversal of reorganisation costs provided for in the 2x05 Financial Statements of Motor Factors. These are costs which the acquirer expects but is not obliged to incur in the future, and are not liabilities at the acquisition date (IFRS 3.11).

(ii) Relating to the joint venture in Auto Parts

The following consolidation adjustment is required in accordance with IAS 28:

	DR €'000	CR €'000
Investment in joint venture	385	
Consolidated retained earnings		385

(Being joint venturer's share of post-acquisition retained earnings of joint venture, i.e. €770k × 50%)

	DR €'000	CR €'000
Consolidated retained earnings	30	
Investment in joint venture		30

(Being elimination of Vorster Limited's share of inter-company profit on inventory: €300k × 1/5 × 50%)

(d) General ledger accounts

(i) Acquisition of Motor Factors

Cost of Control a/c in Motor Factors

	€'000		€'000
Investment in Mot Fact. (€1,500,000 – €25,000)	1,475	OSC	160
		Retained earnings	680
Current tax payable (€180,000 × 80%)	144	Reval surplus (€75,000 × 80%)	60
		Reversal of provision for reorganisation expenses (€90,000 × 80%)	72
		Goodwill (Note (a))	647
	1,619		1,619

Non-controlling Interests in Motor Factors

	€'000		€'000
Income tax payable	36	OSC	40
		Retained earnings	
Bal. to Consolidated SOFP	207	(€850k × 20%)	170
		Revaluation surplus	15
		Reversal of provision for	
		reorganisation expenses	18
	243		243

Retained Earnings of Motor Factors

	€'000		€'000
Cost of control			
(€850k × 80%)	680	Bal. from SOFP	850
Non-controlling interests			
(€850k × 20%)	170		
	850		850

Note (a)

In accordance with IFRS 3, goodwill arising on acquisition is computed as follows (IFRS 3.32):

	€'000
Fair value of consideration paid(€1,500k − €25k)	1,475
Non-controlling interests (1,035 × 20%)	207
	1,682
Less fair value of identifiable net assets acquired	
(1,050k + €75k* − €180k + €90k)	(1,035)
Goodwill	647

*The fair value adjustment is €100k less a deferred tax provision of €25k.

(ii)   Consolidated retained earnings

Consolidated Retained Earnings

	€'000		€'000
Elim. of inter-co. profit on inventory	30	From SOFP of Vorster	2,885
Professional fees	25	50% of post-acq. retained earnings of Auto Parts	385
Bal. to Consolidated SOFP	3,215		
	3,270		3,270

SOLUTION TO
WEBSTER GROUP

Craughwell James & Co.

Memorandum

To: **Pamela Deane**

From: **A. Senior**

Date: **28 February 2x07**

Re: **Webster Group**

Further to our recent meeting I have now had the opportunity to review the issues arising in respect of the audit of the Webster Group for the year ended 31 December 2x06. I will deal with each issue in turn.

Issue (a) – Deferred Tax

Computation of deferred tax balance at 31 December 2x06

	€'m
(i) *Temporary differences relating to the 12.5% corporation tax rate*	
• **Deposit interest** Taxable temporary difference in respect of interest receivable at 31 December 2x06	2.4
• **Intra-group inventory profit** Deductible temporary difference in respect of intra-group profit on inventory (€36m × .25 × .5)	(4.5)

- **Capital allowances**

Net book value at 31 December 2x06	€4,820m
Tax written down value at 31 December 2x06	(€4,420m)
Taxable temporary difference at 31 December 2x06	400
Net taxable temporary differences at 31 December 2x06	397.9

(ii) Temporary differences relating to the 20% capital gains tax rate

	€'m
Land site	
Taxable temporary difference at 31 December 2x06	150
Investment property	
Taxable temporary difference at 31 December 2x06	15
Total taxable temporary differences at 31 December 2x06	165

(iii) Deferred tax computation

Taxable temporary differences of €397.9m @ 12.5%	49.7
Taxable temporary differences of €165m @ 20%	33.0
Deferred tax provision required at 31 December 2x06	82.7
Deferred tax provision at 31 December 2x05	(20.0)
Increase in deferred tax provision at 31 December 2x06	62.7

This increase in deferred tax provision will be charged to the Group state-ment of comprehensive income for the year ended 31 December 2x06. An exception, however, will be that part of the increased provision which relates to the revaluation of the land site. The revaluation surplus on the land site in 2x06 was not recorded in profit or loss, but was instead reflected in other comprehensive income. Thus, the deferred tax charge on the revaluation surplus will similarly be recorded in other comprehensive income.

The amount of the deferred tax provision relating to the land site revalua-tion is computed as the revaluation surplus × CGT rate, i.e. €150m × 20% = €30m.

Journal Entry to reflect the increase in Deferred Tax provision at 31 December 2x06

	DR €'m	CR €'m
Deferred tax charge – SOCI P/L	32.7	
Deferred tax charge – SOCI OCI	30.0	
Deferred tax provision – SOFP		62.7

Issue (b) – Closure of Division

Disposal Group Held for Sale

IFRS 5 states that an entity shall classify a non-current asset (or disposal group) as held for sale if its carrying amount will be recovered principally through a sale transaction rather than through continuing use (IFRS 5.6). The export division appears to qualify under this requirement, as the assets are available for immediate sale, and it is highly probable that their sale will be completed early in 2x07.

The net assets of the export division of First Limited constitute a disposal group and, as they include a non-current asset (i.e. buildings), they should be accounted for under the rules of IFRS 5 (IFRS 5.4).

At the 30 November 2x06 (i.e. the date on which the disposal group is classified as held for sale), the carrying amount of all the assets and liabilities in the disposal group should be measured in accordance with applicable IFRSs. Thus, inventory should be written down from its cost of €30 million to its net realisable value of €26 million, in accordance with IAS 2 (IAS 2.28).

	DR €'m	CR €'m
Cost of sales	4	
Inventory – SOFP		4

(Being reduction of inventory to NRV @ 30 Nov 2x06)

The net assets of the division should now be classified as a disposal group held for sale (IFRS 5.6):

	DR €'m	CR €'m
Disposal group held for sale – current asset	68.6	
Net assets of export division		68.6

(Being classification of net assets of the export division as a disposal group held for sale)

The net assets of the export division should then be measured at fair value less costs to sell (IFRS 5.20). The carrying value of the division's net assets at 30 November (after the inventory adjustment above) amounts to €68.6 million. Fair value less costs to sell is €63.9 million, thus necessitating the following journal adjustment:

	DR €'m	CR €'m
Impairment loss – SOCI P/L	4.7	
Disposal group held for sale – SOFP		4.7

(Being re-measurement of net assets of export division to fair value less costs to sell)

The assets of the export division should be presented separately from other current assets in the consolidated statement of financial position at 31 December 2x06 (IFRS 5.38). It will be appropriate to classify the assets of the export division held for sale under current assets (IFRS 5.3).

The liabilities of the export division should be presented separately from other liabilities in the consolidated statement of financial position (IFRS 5.38).

The assets and liabilities of the export division should *not* be offset and presented as a single amount (IFRS 5.38).

Discontinued Operation

IFRS 5 defines a discontinued operation as a component of an entity that either has been disposed of, or is classified as held for sale. The export division of First Limited is classified as held for sale on 30 November 2x06, and it is therefore a discontinued operation in the 2x06 financial statements.

The following should be presented as a single amount on the face of the consolidated statement of comprehensive income:

- €88 million, being the sum of the post-tax loss of the export division (i.e. €96m – €12m + €4m inventory write down) *plus*

- €4.7 million, being the post-tax loss recognised on the re-measurement of the export division at fair value less costs to sell (IFRS 5.33).

Issue (c) – Interest Costs

IAS 23 requires that costs that are directly attributable to the acquisition, construction or production of a qualifying asset shall be capitalised as part of the cost of that asset (IAS 23.11).

Second Limited has previously written off all interest costs to the statement of comprehensive income. In 2x06, however, due to revised IAS 23 requirements, it has decided to treat interest costs incurred on the construction of a new factory building as part of the cost of the asset.

As all expenditure by Second Limited is assumed to be incurred after the 1 January 2009, retrospective application will apply under IAS 23 *Borrowing Costs,* should the change in treatment constitute a change in accounting policy.

IAS 8 defines *Accounting Policies* as "…the specific principles, bases, conventions, rules and practices applied by an entity in preparing and presenting financial statements" (IAS 8.5). In its *Conceptual Framework* the IASB emphasises the importance of the recognition and measurement of the elements of financial statements.

It is reasonable to assume therefore that a material change in an entity's recognition, measurement basis or presentation of an element of financial statements, such as an asset or expense, is likely to represent a change in accounting policy.

Does Second Ltd's treatment of interest involve a change in:	
Recognition?	Yes
Presentation?	Yes
Measurement basis?	No

In 2x06, interest is being **recognised** as an asset for the first time, and it is being **presented** in the statement of financial position, rather than in the statement of comprehensive income. On this basis, there has been a material change in the manner in which Second Limited prepares and presents its financial statements. The capitalisation of interest relating to the construction of the new factory building is therefore a change in accounting policy.

In accordance with IAS 23, capitalisation should commence when expenditures are being incurred, borrowing costs are being incurred and activities that are necessary to prepare the asset for its intended use or sale are in progress (IAS 23.20). In the case of Second Limited, this date is the 1 January 2x05.

IAS 23 also requires that borrowing costs should **not** be capitalised when construction is interrupted, as such costs are costs of holding partially completed assets and do not qualify for capitalisation (IAS 23.24). In respect of Second Limited, therefore, interest costs incurred between 1 April 2x06 and 30 June 2x06 should be expensed to profit or loss.

Capitalisation should cease when substantially all of the activities necessary to prepare the asset for its intended use or sale are complete, which in Second Limited's case is 30 September 2x06 (IAS 23.25).

General overheads are **not** a directly attributable cost relating to the construction of the factory building by Second Limited, and therefore related borrowing costs should not be capitalised.

Borrowing costs to be capitalised in 2x05

Item	Cost €'m	Timescale from commencement on 1 January 2x05 to 31 December 2x05	Annual Equivalent €'m
Site clearance*	46	12 months	46
Building materials	120	9 months	90
Direct labour and production overheads	60	7 months	35
Total			171

*Although site clearance is completed by 31 March 2x05, the site is not suitable for its intended use until construction work is completed on 30 September 2x06.

Therefore, borrowing costs relating to the site clearance work should continue to be capitalised until 30 September 2x06 (IAS 23.27).

The interest rate was 7% (bank base rate + 2%) from 1 January to 31 December 2x05. When this is applied to the eligible costs of €171 million, the borrowing costs to be capitalised amount to €12 million.

The following journal entry is therefore required:

	DR €'m	CR €'m
Land and buildings	12	
Retained earnings		12

(Being correction of interest costs expensed in 2x05, which are now capitalised by means of retrospective adjustment)

Borrowing costs to be capitalised in 2x06

Item	Cost €'m	Timescale from 1 January 2x06 to 30 September 2x06 (excluding 3-month suspension period)	Annual Equivalent €'m
Site clearance	46	6 months	23
Bldg mats (20x5)	120	6 months	60
Bldg mats (2x06)	140	3 months	35
Direct lab. & prod. o/h's (2x05)	60	6 months	30
Direct lab. & prod. o/h's (2x06)	100	3 months	25
Total			173

The interest rate was 8% (bank base rate + 2%) from 1 January to 30 September 2x06. When this is applied to the relevant costs of €173m, the borrowing costs to be capitalised amount to €13.84m (i.e. €173m × 8%).

The following journal entry is therefore required.

	DR €'m	CR €'m
Land and buildings	13.84	
Finance costs – SOCI P/L		13.84

(Being correction of interest costs expensed in 2x06, which are now capitalised)

Accounting Policy Note

During 2x06, Second Limited changed its accounting policy for the treatment of borrowing costs that are directly attributable to the construction of a new factory building. In previous periods, Second Limited had written off such costs as an expense. Second Limited has now decided to include these costs as part of qualifying assets, as this treatment is required in accordance with the revised rules of IAS 23 *Borrowing Costs.*

Issue (d) – Revenue

Sales on a deferred payment basis
Revenue should be measured at the fair value of the consideration received or receivable (IAS 18.9). When the inflow of cash or cash equivalents is deferred, the fair value of the consideration may be less than the nominal amount of cash received or receivable. When the arrangement effectively constitutes a financing transaction, the fair value of the consideration is determined by discounting all future receipts (IAS 18.11).

Thus, the sales made by First Limited on a deferred payment basis should be discounted to derive their fair value. As First Limited gives a 10% discount to cash customers, this would appear to represent an appropriate discount rate in this case.

The discounted value of deferred payment sales made in 2x06 can therefore be measured as €340 million/1.1 = €309 million.

The deferred payment sales will therefore be recorded as follows by First Limited in its 2x06 financial statements:

	DR €'m	CR €'m
Trade receivables	309	
Revenue		309

On the assumption that First Limited receives payment for the goods in 2x07, the following accounting entries will be made in the year ending 31 December 2x07:

	DR €'m	CR €'m
Bank	340	
Trade receivables		309
Interest income – SOCI P/L		31

Customer warranties

In accordance with IAS 37, it will be necessary to recognise a provision for the return of goods by customers (IAS 37.39). For those goods that can be resold after their return, the provision that is required can be computed as follows:

- €340m × 4% × 90% × 25% = €3.06 million

The provision that is required for goods which will have a zero resale value is calculated as follows:

- €340m × 4% × 10% × 100% = €1.36 million

Therefore, the following journal entry is required:

	DR €'m	CR €'m
Provision for customer warranty – SOCI P/L	4.42	
Provision for customer warranty – SOFP		4.42

Issue (e) – Financial instruments

(i) *Loan stock*

IFRS 9 *Financial Instruments* states that, after initial recognition, financial assets should be measured at fair value or amortised cost (IFRS 9.5.2.1). A financial asset should be measured at amortised cost if both of the following conditions are met:

(a) the asset is held in order to collect contractual cash flows; and
(b) the cash flows are solely payments of principal and interest.

The loan stock purchased by Second Limited satisfies these conditions, and it should be accounted for at amortised cost as follows:

	DR €'000	CR €'000
Financial asset	10,000	
Bank		10,000
(Being purchase of loan stock on 1 January 2x06)		
Financial asset	1,000	
Interest receivable – SOCI P/L		1,000
(Being interest @ 10% for y/e 31 December 2x06)		
Financial asset	1,100	
Interest receivable – SOCI P/L		1,100

(Being interest @ 10% for y/e
  31 December 2x07
  i.e. (10m + €1m) × 10%)		

Financial asset	1,210	
Interest receivable – SOCI P/L		1,210

(Being interest @ 10% for y/e
  31 December 2x08
  i.e. (10m + €1m + €1.1m) × 10%)		

Bank	13,310	
Financial asset		13,310
(Being encashment of loan stock at maturity)		

(ii) *Purchase and disposal of shares*

IFRS 9 *Financial Instruments* states that a financial asset should be measured at fair value unless it is measured at amortised cost (IFRS 9.4.1.4). IFRS 9 also requires that a gain or loss should be recognised in profit or loss for most financial assets measured at fair value (IFRS 9.5.7.1).

Therefore, the purchase and disposal by Second Limited of shares in Smile Plc should be accounted for as follows:

	DR €'m	CR €'m
Financial asset	85,000	
Bank		85,000

(Being purchase of equity shares
  on 1 January 2x06)

Investment income receivable – SOFP	3,000	
Investment income – SOCI P/L		3,000

(Being dividend income due from
  Smile Plc at 31 December 2x06)

Financial asset	12,000	
Revaluation gain – SOCI P/L		12,000

(Being remeasurement of equity shares at
  fair value at 31 December 2x06)

Bank	103,000	
Financial asset		97,000
Gain on disposal of shares – SOCI P/L		6,000

(Being gain on disposal of shares in
  February 2x07)

SOLUTION TO
THE HAYWARD GROUP

Parker Russell & Co. Chartered Accountants

Accounting issues relating to the Hayward Holdings Group

Report dated 31 March 2x10

(a) Business Rationalisation

(b) Head Office Building

(c) Flexible Packaging

(d) New Opportunity

Mr Jim Hayward,
Chairman,
Hayward Holdings Limited,
Any Street,
ANYTOWN
31 March 2x10

Report on accounting issues in respect of 2x09 Audit

Dear Mr Hayward,

Further to our recent discussions, please find enclosed a copy of our report which sets out the appropriate accounting treatment and disclosure requirements regarding various matters which have arisen in respect of the 2x09 Audit of the various Hayward Group companies.

I look forward to discussing these issues with you in detail when we meet next week.

Yours sincerely

A. N. Auditor

Issue (a) – Business Rationalisation

(i) *Restructuring provision*

In accordance with IAS 37 *Provisions, Contingent Liabilities and Contingent Assets,* a provision should only be recognised when (IAS 37.14):

- An entity has a present obligation (legal or constructive) as a result of a past event;
- It is probable that an outflow of resources embodying economic benefits will be required to settle the obligation; *and*
- A reliable estimate can be made of the amount of the obligation.

In terms of restructuring, a constructive obligation to restructure arises only when an entity (IAS 37.72):

- has a detailed formal plan for the restructuring, *and*
- has raised a valid expectation in those affected that it will carry out the restructuring by starting to implement that plan, or announcing its main features to those affected by it.

The standard goes on to state that a management or board decision to restructure does **not** give rise to a constructive obligation unless the entity has (before the end of the reporting period):

- started to implement the restructuring plan; or
- announced the main features of the plan to those affected by it in a sufficiently specific manner to raise a valid expectation to them that the entity will carry out the restructuring (IAS 37.75).

In this case, although Hayward Adhesives has developed a plan that has been approved in principle by the Board of Directors, the plan remains confidential and has neither been announced publicly nor discussed with those who may be affected by it. Consequently, in accordance with IAS 37, no provision should be made in the 2x09 Financial Statements for the costs of implementation of the Exit Plan.

(ii) *Non-current assets (or disposal groups) classified as held for sale, in accordance with IFRS 5*

A non-current asset (or disposal group) should be classified as held for sale if its carrying amount will be recovered principally through a sale transaction rather than through continuing use (IFRS 5. 6).

For this to be the case, the asset (or disposal group) must be available for immediate sale in its present condition, and its sale must be highly probable (IFRS 5.7). A sale is highly probable if management is committed to a plan to sell the asset (or disposal group), and an active programme to locate a buyer and complete the plan has been initiated. Further, the asset (or disposal group) must be actively marketed for sale at a price that is reasonable in relation to its current fair value. In addition, the sale completion should normally be expected within one year from the date of classification (IFRS 5.8).

The above conditions appear to be satisfied in respect of the continuous printing equipment used by Hayward Adhesives, which constitutes a disposal group under IFRS 5 (i.e. a group of assets to be disposed of together). The equipment is available for sale, management is committed to a plan to sell (Board Decision in October 2x09), a buyer has been located (in the Far East), the price is reasonable in relation to the current fair value of the equipment, and the sale is expected to be completed within one year (the Exit Plan is expected to take six months to complete).

Thus, in accordance with IFRS 5, the equipment should be reclassified as a disposal group held for sale. IFRS 5 requires that, immediately before its initial classification as held for sale, the carrying amounts of a disposal group should be measured in accordance with applicable IFRSs (IFRS 5.18).

Applying the requirements of IAS 16 *Property, Plant & Equipment*, in respect of assets being measured under the cost model of IAS 16, such assets should be carried at cost less any accumulated depreciation and any accumulated impairment losses. To ascertain if an impairment loss has occurred in respect of the equipment of Hayward Adhesives, it will be necessary to compare its carrying value and its recoverable amount:

- Carrying value €2 million
- Value in use – very limited value, not stated
- Net selling price €900,000.

The equipment has a recoverable amount (higher of value in use and fair value less costs to sell, as per IAS 16.6) of €900,000, which is less than its carrying value of €2 million. Consequently, an impairment write-down is required, and the equipment should then be reclassified as a disposal group held for sale. The following journal entries are required:

	DR €'000	CR €'000
Impairment write-down – SOCI P/L	1,100	
Plant & equipment		1,100
(Being impairment write-down of equipment to its recoverable amount)		
Disposal group held for sale – SOFP	900	
Plant & equipment		900
(Being reclassification of equipment as a non-current asset held for sale)		

(iii)   *Discontinued operation*

Definition
IFRS 5 defines a discontinued operation as a component of an entity that either, has been disposed of, or is classified as held for sale, and:

- represents a separate major line of business or geographical area of operations
- is part of a single co-ordinated plan to dispose of a separate major line of business or geographical area of operations, *or*
- is a subsidiary acquired exclusively with a view to resale (IFRS Appendix A).

The Business Adhesives' division is a component of the Hayward Group, being a separate major line of business. The net assets of this division represent a disposal group held for sale (see (ii) above), and the Business Adhesives' division therefore qualifies as a discontinued operation in accordance with Appendix A of IFRS 5.

Presentation
The following should be presented as a single amount on the face of the statement of comprehensive income of Hayward Forms, and that of the Group (IFRS 5.33):

- The sum of the post-tax profit or loss of the discontinued adhesives' operation

because After tax loss

- The post-tax gain or loss recognised on the measurement of the equipment at fair value less costs to sell (i.e. €1.1m adjusted for tax).

Disclosure
Detailed disclosure of the following information must be provided in the financial statements of Hayward Forms Limited, and those of the Group:

– Revenue, expenses, pre-tax profit or loss, and related income taxes. This can be provided either in the notes, or on the face of the statement of comprehensive income, in a separate section from continuing operations. Such disclosure must cover the current and all prior periods presented in the financial statements (IFRS 5.33).

Issue (b) – Head Office Building

On 31 December 2x09, Hayward Holdings entered into a binding agreement to sell its head office building to Alpha Investments Ltd for €2 million. The agreement includes back-to-back put-and-call options for transfer of title to the building back to Hayward Holdings at a price calculated on the basis of €2 million plus indexation at the bank base lending rate. This option will automatically activate at the end of five years. Hayward will pay a rent to Alpha Investments, based on the average daily bank rate +5%.

In accounting for this, and other transactions, the IASB Framework Document requires Hayward Holdings to reflect the substance of the transactions into which it has entered. The substance of this transaction may be determined by considering the position of both buyer and seller, together with their motives for agreeing to its various terms. Ownership of an asset will generally confer the following risks and benefits:

Benefits
- the benefit of any expected increase in the value of the asset; and
- benefits arising from use or development of the asset

Risks
- the risk of unexpected variation in the value of the asset
- the risk of obsolescence.

In this case, following the transfer of the building to Alpha Investments Ltd on 31 December 2x09, it would appear that the risks and rewards of ownership continue to be vested in Hayward Holdings, who continue to bear any obsolescence risk, and who will benefit from any increase in the value of the building. It is also apparent that Alpha Investments Ltd is getting a lender's return from the funds advanced to Hayward Holdings. This return is linked to the bank interest rate, rather than to any change in the value of the building.

Consequently, the substance of this transaction is that Hayward Holdings has obtained a secured loan from Alpha Investments Ltd. Hayward should continue to recognise the building in its financial statements, and record the proceeds received from Alpha Investments as a liability. Interest should be accrued over the period of the advance. The building should continue to be depreciated, and assessed annually for any indication of impairment.

The transaction should be reflected as follows in the financial statements of Hayward Holdings (and of the Group) at 31 December 2x09.

	DR €'000	CR €'000
Bank ↑	2,000	
Loan to Alpha		2,000

(Being proceeds received in respect of securitised loan)

Related Party Implications

Hayward Holdings and Alpha Investments Ltd are both controlled by Jim Hayward, and are therefore deemed to be related parties by IAS 24. The following information should be disclosed in the financial statements of Hayward Holdings and those of the Group (IAS 24.17):

- The nature of the related party relationship (subject to common control)
- Details of the transaction (securitised loan from Alpha Investments)
- Outstanding balances (amount of €2 million loan + interest which remains outstanding)
- Any other information necessary for an understanding of the potential effect of the relationship on the financial statements.

Issue (c) – Flexible Packaging

(i)   *Danish customer*
Hayward Flexo has included in its sales for the year an item that was not physically despatched until after the year end.

IAS 18 states that revenue arising from the sale of goods should be recognised when all of the following conditions have been satisfied: (IAS 18.14)

- the seller has transferred to the buyer the significant risks and rewards of ownership;
- the seller retains neither continuing managerial involvement to the degree usually associated with ownership nor effective control over the goods sold;
- the amount of revenue can be measured reliably;
- it is probable that the economic benefits associated with the transaction will flow to the seller; and
- the costs incurred or to be incurred in respect of the transaction can be measured reliably.

As Danobuy had stated that it did not wish to receive delivery of the goods until after their year end on 31 January 2x10, it is clear that no sale had taken place at 31 December 2x09.

Thus, Hayward Flexo had not transferred the significant risks and rewards of ownership to Danobuy at the year-end, and no sale should be recorded in the financial statements at that date.

The correct treatment is to retain the product in finished goods inventory, and invoice the goods when they are dispatched in February 2x10.

IAS 2 states that inventory should be held at the lower of cost and net realisable value (IAS 2.9). In this instance cost will be lower, and should be calculated as follows:

	€'000
Selling price	400
Less profit content @ 70%	(280)
Material cost	120
Add production overhead @ 15%	18
Inventory @ cost	138

The following journal entries are required:

	DR €'000	CR €'000
Revenue – SOCI P/L	400	
Trade receivables		400
(Being reversal of initial transaction)		
Inventory – SOFP ↑	138	
Cost of sales		138
(Being inclusion of goods in inventory @ 31 December 2x09)		

(ii) *French customer*

During the year Hayward Flexo has sold product to a customer in France which has, prior to the year-end, proved to be defective.

In accordance with IAS 37, a provision should be recognised when an entity has a present obligation as a result of a past event, it is probable that it will have to pay to settle it, and a reasonable estimate can be made as to the costs of settlement (IAS 37.14).

Applying the recognition criteria of IAS 37 to this instance:

- *present obligation* – Hayward Flexo guaranteed its product for the intended use, but a batch was found to be defective for that use. It appears almost certain that Hayward Flexo will have to provide a refund on the sale.
- *past event* – the supply of goods took place in November 2x09
- *reasonable estimate of expenditure required to settle* – the customer has indicated that they will not accept substitute goods to replace those which have proved defective. In order to settle the matter, therefore, Hayward Flexo is likely to have to write off the original debt, as well as meeting the costs incurred by Supermarche.

A provision of €600,000 is therefore required.

The ink supplier has indicated that it will cover part of the costs incurred by Hayward Flexo, as it was partly responsible for the problems that have arisen. IAS 37 states that, where some or all of the expenditure required to settle a provision is expected to be reimbursed by another party, the reimbursement should be recognised only when it is virtually certain to be received if the entity (Hayward Flexo) settles the obligation (IAS 37.53). In this case, the ink supplier has offered in writing to reimburse Hayward Flexo for 50% of the costs of settling the matter.

Per IAS 37, the amount recognised for the reimbursement should be treated as a separate asset (IAS 37.53). The expense, in the statement of comprehensive income, relating to a provision, may however be presented net of the amount recognised for a reimbursement (IAS 37.54).

The following journal entry is required in respect of the 2x09 financial statements of Hayward Flexo:

	DR €'000	CR €'000
Receivable for reimbursement – SOFP	300	
Increase in provision for product liability – SOCI P/L	300	
Provision for product liability – SOFP		600
(Being provision established in respect of product liability claim)		

Issue (d) – New Opportunity

From an accounting perspective, the key question is how should the investment in Virtual Inc. Ltd be presented in the Group financial statements. There are a number of alternatives:

- a simple investment
- an associate
- a joint venture
- a subsidiary.

A simple investment implies a limited interest, which does not give the investor significant influence. The 25% stake purchased by Hayward Holdings appears to provide the Group with significant influence over the policies of Virtual Inc., particularly as the Hayward Group has two members on that company's board.

For the investment to qualify as a subsidiary, the investor has to control the investee (IFRS 10) – in this case the other shareholder retains a 75% stake, and therefore Hayward Holdings could not be said to control Virtual Inc.

It is clear therefore that Virtual Inc. is either an associate or a joint venture of the Hayward Group. An associate is defined as an entity over which the investor has significant influence, and that is neither a subsidiary nor an interest in a joint venture (IAS 28.3). A joint venture is a joint arrangement whereby the parties that have joint control of the arrangement have rights to the net assets.

A distinction between an associate and a joint venture is that in a joint venture no party can control the investee company on its own. In this case, there does not appear to be any contractual agreement as to control, and control has been retained by Dave Foster, who still retains 75% of the share capital of Virtual Inc.

On the basis of the above analysis, it is clear that Virtual Inc. is an associate of the Hayward Group.

Accounting for Virtual Inc.

(i)   *Separate financial statements of Hayward Holdings Limited*
The shares purchased in Virtual Inc. will initially be recorded as an investment at cost. Subsequently, Hayward Holdings Limited will record dividends received from Virtual Inc., along with any impairment in that company's value. The following entry, which has already been made by Hayward Holdings Limited, accurately reflects the purchase of its shares in Virtual Inc.

	DR €'000	CR €'000
Investment in Virtual Inc. Ltd	7,300	
Bank		7,300

(ii)   *Group financial statements*   → Now IFRS 10

In accordance with IAS 28 *Investments in Associates and Joint Ventures*, Virtual Inc. should be accounted for in the financial statements of the Hayward Group using the equity method (IAS 28.16). It should initially be recognised at cost, and adjusted thereafter for the post-acquisition change in the investor's share of net assets of the investee. The profit or loss of the investor should include the investor's share of the profit or loss of the investee (IAS 28.10). Investments in associates accounted for using the equity method should be classified as non-current assets (IAS 28.15).

Thus, in the financial statements of the Hayward Group, the following journal entries are required in respect of the investment in Virtual Inc.:

	DR €'000	CR €'000
Investment in Associate	7,300	
Investments		7,300
(Being re-classification of investment)		
Investment in Associate	37.5	
Share of profit of associate – consolidated SOCI P/L		37.5
(Being group share of post-acquisition earnings of Virtual Inc. – see note 1)		

Note 1: On the assumption that the profits of Virtual Inc. are earned evenly over the year, profit earned in the period 1 October – 31 December 2x09 is €37,500 (i.e. €600,000 × 3/12 × 25%).

[handwritten margin notes:]

initial recognition @ cost

profit   600
      25%
      ____
      3/12

= 37.5

SOLUTION TO
BLACK BAY BOATS

ABC & Co Chartered Accountants

Memorandum

To: **D. Bosse**

From: **A. Senior**

Date: **20 March 2x13**

Re: **Black Bay Boats Limited**

Further to your recent e-mail I have now had the opportunity to review the issues arising in respect of the audit of Black Bay Boats Limited for the year ended 31 December 2x12. I will deal with each issue in turn.

(1)   Investment in Pleasure Craft Inc.

There are a number of accounting and disclosure issues linked to the investment in Pleasure Craft Inc. These include:

- How should the investment be accounted for?

- What value/cost should be placed on the investment, and what fair value adjustments are required to determine the net assets of Pleasure Craft Inc.?

- What is the value of goodwill arising on acquisition?

- Disclosures required.

I will deal with each issue in turn: -

(a)   *How should the investment be accounted for?*
IFRS 10 Consolidated Financial Statements, defines a subsidiary as an entity that is controlled by another entity (IFRS 10, Appendix A). An investor controls an investee when the investor is exposed to, or has rights to, variable returns, and has the ability to affect those returns through its power over the investee (IFRS 10, Appendix A).

In this case therefore, at the time of the first investment of 10%, Pleasure Craft Inc. would *not* have been treated as a subsidiary. At 30 September 2x12 the total investment has increased to 50%, although a majority of the voting rights are still not controlled, as the company's equity is split 50:50 between Black Bay Boats and Bill & Ted Powers. In this case Jim Kennedy has been appointed MD, and the Pleasure Craft operation is being managed as part of Black Bay Boats, through the same management structures and using the same systems. It is also noteworthy that Bill and Ted Powers have withdrawn from the management of the business. Clearly, therefore, Black Bay Boats had rights, on 30 September 2x12, that gave it the ability to direct the activities of Pleasure Craft Inc.

One can conclude that Black Bay Boats exercises control over Pleasure Craft Inc., and that the latter company became a subsidiary at 30 September 2x12.

(b)   *What value should be placed on the investment?*
The cost of each investment was as follows:

31 March 2x12 – 10% of share capital for $1m

30 September 2x12 – 40% of the share capital for $5m.

At each date the $:€ rate was 1.60:1, which means that the total cost in € was €3.75 million and this is correctly accounted for in the draft financial statements of Black Bay Boats Limited.

Fair Value Adjustments
IFRS 3 requires that the consideration transferred in a business combination shall be measured at fair value, which shall be calculated as the sum of:

- the acquisition date fair value of assets transferred by the acquirer
- liabilities incurred, and
- equity interests issued by the acquirer (IFRS 3.37).

I note the following from the background papers supplied:

- A property valuation report dated 1 January 2x12. This had been undertaken by Professional Valuers acting on behalf of Pleasure Craft Inc. which indicated that the company's primary property has increased by $1m in value compared to its carrying amount in the financial statements of Pleasure Craft Inc. The previous valuation was carried out in 2x07.

- A major customer of Pleasure Craft Inc. filed for bankruptcy on 1 September 2x12. At that time he owed the company $200,000. It is believed that nothing will be recovered from the bad debt.

- The net assets of Pleasure Craft Inc. must be adjusted to reflect these items.

	1 January '12 $000	31 March '12 $000	30 Sept '12 $000	31 December '12 $000
Net assets per Accounts	9,000	9,280	9,840	10,120
Fair value adjustments	+1,000	+1,000	+1,000 −200	+1,000 −200
Adjusted Net Assets	10,000	10,280	10,640	10,920

IFRS 3 also requires that, where a business combination is achieved in stages, the acquirer must remeasure its previously held equity interest at acquisition date fair value (IFRS 3.42). The resulting gain or loss, if any, should be recognised in profit or loss (IFRS 3.42).

As the adjusted net asset amounts represent fair value, the value of Pleasure Craft Inc. will have increased to $10,640,000 between Black Bay Boats' initial investment of 10% on 31 March 2x12 and its additional investment of 40% on 30 September 2x12.

Thus, remeasuring the 10% stake acquired by Black Bay Boats on the 31 March 2x12 will give rise to a fair value of $1,064,000 at acquisition date (i.e. 30 September 2x12). At an exchange rate of €1 = $1.6, this amounts to €665,000. This represents a gain of €40,000 on the initial cost of investment (i.e. €625,000), and it will be recorded as follows in the Group financial statements of Black Bay Boats:

	DR €'000	CR €'000
Investment in Pleasure Craft	40	
Gain on restatement of investment – SOCI P/L		40

(c)   Goodwill

IFRS 3 requires that goodwill is measured as the excess of (1) over (2) (IFRS 3.32):

(1)   the aggregate of:

   (i)   the consideration transferred (€3,125,000) — i.e. $5m/1.6

   (ii)   the amount of any non-controlling interest in the acquiree (€3,325,000) – i.e. ($10,640,000/1.6) x 50%

   (iii)   in a business combination achieved in stages, the acquisition date fair value of the acquirer's previously held equity interest in the acquiree (€665,000) – i.e. ($10,640,000/1.6) x 10%

(2)   the net of the acquisition-date amounts of the identifiable assets acquired and the liabilities assumed (measured in accordance with IFRS 3) (€6,650,000) – i.e. $10,640,000/1.6

Thus, goodwill = (€3,125,000 + €3,325,000 + €665,000)
– €6,650,000

= €465,000

(d)   Accounting record of acquisition of shares in Pleasure Craft Inc.

   (i)   Separate Financial Statements of Black Bay Boats

	DR €'000	CR €'000
Investment in Pleasure Craft Inc.	625	
Bank		625
(Being purchase of 10% of Pleasure Craft)		
Investment in Pleasure Craft Inc.	3,125	
Bank		3,125
(Being purchase of 40% of Pleasure Craft)		

(ii)   Group Financial Statements of Black Bay Boats

	DR €'000	CR €'000
Investment in Pleasure Craft	625	
Bank		625
(Being purchase of 10% stake in Pleasure Craft Inc.)		
Investment in Pleasure Craft	40	
Gain on restatement of Investment – SOCI P/L		40
(Being remeasurement of previously held equity interest at acquisition date fair value)		
Net assets ($10,640/1.6)	6,650	
Goodwill	465	
Bank		3,125
Non-controlling interests (€6,650k x 50%)		3,325
Investment in Pleasure Craft (€625k + €40k)		665
(Being purchase of 40% stake in Pleasure Craft Inc.)		

(e)   Disclosure

Appendix B of IFRS 3 requires that an acquirer shall disclose specific information for each business combination that occurs during the reporting period (IFRS 3, Appendix B.64).

The following disclosure note, relating to the acquisition of Pleasure Craft Inc., is based on the illustrative examples in IFRS 3:

Para. ref.		€'000
B64 (a-d)	On 31 March 2x12 Black Bay Boats acquired 10% of the outstanding ordinary shares of Pleasure Craft. On 30 September Black Bay Boats acquired 40% of Pleasure Craft and obtained control of that company by virtue of its control over policy and decision-making. As a result of the acquisition, Black Bay Boats has achieved penetration into the lucrative US market.	
B64 (e)	The goodwill of €465,000 arising from the acquisition, consists largely of the increased market opportunities from combining the operations of Black Bay Boats and Pleasure Craft.	
B64 (k)	The following table summarises the consideration paid for Pleasure Craft and the amounts of the assets acquired and liabilities assumed at the acquisition date, as well as the fair value at the acquisition date of the non-controlling interest in Pleasure Craft:	
	At 30 September 2x12 **Consideration**	
B64 (f)(i)	Cash	3,125
B64 p (i)	Fair value of Black Bay Boat's equity interest in Pleasure Craft before the business combination	665 3,790
B64 (i)	Recognised amounts of identifiable assets acquired and liabilities assumed	6,650
B64 (o)(i)	Non-controlling interest in Pleasure Craft Goodwill	(3,325) 465 3,790

(2) Foreign Currency Loan

A foreign currency loan is a monetary liability, as defined by IAS 21 *The Effects of Changes in Foreign Exchange Rates*. Under the procedures set out in IAS 21, exchange gains or losses on foreign currency borrowings would normally be reported as part of a company's profit or loss, and would flow through into the consolidated statement of comprehensive income.

Separate Financial Statements of Black Bay Boats
IAS 21 however states that the rules of IAS 39 apply to hedge accounting for foreign currency items (IAS 21.27). The foreign currency loan may, in the case of Black Bay Boats, be regarded as a hedge against exchange rate movements in respect of its investment in Pleasure Craft Inc.
IAS 39 defines a cash flow hedge as ". . . a hedge of the exposure to variability in cash flows that:

(i) is attributable to a particular risk associated with a recognised asset or liability or a highly probable forecast transaction, *and*
(ii) could affect profit or loss." (IAS 39.86(b))

The $ loan taken out by Black Bay Boats to finance its acquisition of shares in Pleasure Craft Inc. appears to qualify as a cash flow hedge. IAS 39 stipulates that a cash flow hedge which meets the qualifying conditions should be accounted for as follows (IAS 39.96):
The separate component of equity associated with the hedged item is adjusted to the lesser of the following:

- the cumulative gain or loss on the hedging instrument (i.e. the $ loan) from inception of the hedge; *and*
- the cumulative change in fair value of the expected future cash flows of the hedged item (i.e. investment in Pleasure Craft Inc.).

Any remaining gain or loss on the hedging instrument (that is not an effective hedge) is recognised in profit or loss.
Therefore, Black Bay Boats should denominate its investment in Pleasure Inc. in $, and compute the exchange gain/loss at the end of each accounting period, and the exchange gains or losses on the borrowings should then be offset, as other comprehensive income, against these exchange differences.

This treatment can be reflected as follows:

	$US	Rate @ acq'n	€'000	Rate @ y/e	€'000
Investment	6,000	1.6	3,750	2.0	3,000
Borrowings	3,000	1.6	1,875	2.0	1,500

This means that the reduction in the fair value of the investment can be off-set against the reduction in the carrying value of the loan. The adjustment is restricted to the amount of the gain on the loan of €375,000.

	DR €'000	CR €'000
Loss on translation of investment – SOCI OCI	375	
Investment		375
Foreign currency loan	375	
Gain on translation of loan – SOCI OCI		375

(Being $ loan used as cash flow hedge to cover $ investment)

Group Financial Statements
Hedges of a net investment in a foreign operation should be accounted for in a similar way to cash flow hedges.

(3) Revaluation of Showroom

IAS 16 permits a choice between a cost model and a revaluation model in respect of property, plant and equipment (IAS 16.29). It is clear that, in respect of its showroom property, Black Bay Boats has opted for the revaluation model.

Revaluation gains should be recognised in profit or loss only to the extent (after adjusting for subsequent depreciation) that they reverse revaluation losses that were previously recognised in profit or loss in respect of the same asset. All other revaluation gains should be recognised in other comprehensive income and accumulated in equity under the heading of revaluation surplus (IAS 16.39).

Where a revaluation gain reverses a revaluation loss that was previously recognised in profit or loss, the gain recognised in profit or loss is reduced by the amount of depreciation that would have been charged had the loss previously taken to the statement of comprehensive income not been recognised in the first place. This is to achieve the same overall effect that would have been reached had the original downward revaluation not occurred.

In this situation it is necessary to consider the following information:

- The company has been trading for 13 years, and that the show-room would have been bought at the date of inception. It is assumed therefore that the year of purchase was 2x00.
- The cost of the showroom was €6.25 million.
- A full year's depreciation is charged in the year of purchase.

On the basis that the showroom was depreciated at 2% on a straight line basis, the following journal entries would have been made up to the time of the first revaluation:

	DR €'000	CR €'000
Depreciation expense – SOCI P/L	125	
Accumulated depreciation		125
(Being annual depreciation from 2x00–2x09 inclusive)		

Consequently, the NBV of the showroom at 31 December 2x09, prior to the first revaluation, was €5 million (€6.25m − €1.25m).

The following is a summary of subsequent events:

		€'000
2x09:	Net book value at 31 December 2x09	5,000
2x10:	Asset write-down	(2,000)
		3,000
	Depreciation for year (€3 million/40 years)	(75)
	NBV at 31 December 2x10	2,925
2x11:	Depreciation for year	(75)
	NBV at 31 December 2x11	2,850
2x12:	Depreciation for year	(75)
		2,775
	Revaluation gain	3,225
	Valuation at 31 December 2x12	6,000

The above amendments 2x10–2x12 will require the following journal entries:

		DR €'000	CR €'000
2x10:	Impairment loss – SOCI P/L	2,000	
	PPE		2,000
	(Being write down of showroom to €3 million)		
	Depreciation expense – SOCI P/L	75	
	Accumulated depreciation		75
	(Being depreciation on showroom for 2x10)		
2x11:	Depreciation expense – SOCI P/L	75	
	Accumulated depreciation		75
	(Being depreciation on showroom for 2x11)		
2x12:	Depreciation expense – SOCI P/L	75	
	Accumulated depreciation		75
	(Being depreciation on showroom for 2x12)		
	Accumulated depreciation	225	
	PPE		225
	(Being reversal of accumulated depreciation on revaluation of showroom)		
	PPE	3,225	
	Reversal of previous impairment loss – SOCI P/L*		1,850
	Revaluation surplus – SOCI OCI		1,375
	(Being revaluation of showroom)		

* Reversal of previous impairment loss

The reversal of the previous impairment loss is restricted as follows:

	€'000
Previous impairment loss charged to profit or loss	2,000
Less additional depreciation that would have been charged had the impairment write-down not taken place: i.e. (3 years × (€125,000 – €75,000)) =	(150)
	1,850

Disclosure

If items of property, plant and equipment have been revalued, the following information should be disclosed (IAS 16.77):

   (i) the effective date of the revaluation

   (ii) whether an independent valuer was involved

   (iii) for each revalued class of property, plant and equipment, the carrying amount that would have been recognised had the assets been carried under the cost model

   (iv) the revaluation surplus, indicating the change for the period and any restrictions on the distribution of the balance to shareholders.

(4) Black Bay Boats: Motor Craft

In respect of the craft held from Baggio, although the deposit has been recorded in the financial statements, the craft and the corresponding trade creditor have not. In its Conceptual Framework, the IASB stipulates that entities should reflect the substance of transactions in their financial statements. It is necessary to consider whether, on this basis, Black Bay Boats has correctly treated the Baggio craft held at the year end.

Consignment inventory is inventory held by one party (the 'dealer') but legally owned by another (the 'manufacturer'), on terms that give the dealer the right to sell the inventory in the normal course of its business or, at its option, to return it unsold to the legal owner.

The inventory may be physically located on the premises of the dealer, or held at another site nearby. The arrangement has a number of commercial advantages for both parties: the dealer is able to hold or have faster access to a wider range of inventory than might otherwise be practicable, and the manufacturer can avoid a build-up on its premises by moving it closer to the point of sale. Both parties benefit from the greater sales potential of the arrangement.

The main features of a consignment inventory arrangement are as follows:

   (a) The manufacturer delivers goods to the dealer, but legal title does not pass until one of a number of events takes place (e.g. the dealer has held the goods for a specified period, adopts them by using them as demonstration models, or sells them to a third party). Until such a crystallising event, the dealer is entitled to return the goods to the manufacturer, or the manufacturer is able to require their return or insist that they are passed to another dealer.

(b) Once legal title passes, the transfer price becomes payable by the dealer. This price may be fixed at the date goods are delivered to the dealer, it may vary with the period between delivery and transfer of title, or it may be the manufacturer's list price at the date of transfer of title.

(c) The dealer may also be required to pay a deposit to the manufacturer, or to pay the latter a display or financing charge. This deposit or charge may be fixed for a period (e.g. one year) or may fluctuate.

(d) Other terms of the arrangement will usually cover items such as inspection and access rights of the manufacturer, and responsibility for damage, loss or theft and related insurance. These are usually of minor importance in determining the accounting treatment.

In order to determine if the inventory is consignment inventory, it is necessary to identify whether the dealer (i.e. Black Bay Boats) has access to the benefits of the inventory, and exposure to the risks inherent in those benefits.

Where it is concluded that the inventory **is** in substance an asset of the dealer, it should be recognised on the dealer's statement of financial position, together with a corresponding liability to the manufacturer. Any deposit should be deducted from the liability and the excess classified as a trade creditor.

Where it is concluded that the inventory is **not** in substance an asset of the dealer, it should not be included on the dealer's statement of financial position until the transfer of title has crystallised. Any deposit should be included under 'other current assets'.

The latter position would appear to apply in respect of the craft held by Black Bay Boats at the year end. The price charged by Baggio remains variable until settled in full. Additionally, Baggio appears to be entitled to arrange for the transfer/return of the craft without penalty. Therefore, the craft should **not** be brought into the books of Black Bay

Boats at this stage. The following journal entry is required in respect of the deposit which has been paid:

	DR €'000	CR €'000
Trade and other receivables	100	
Trade payables		100

(Being correction of entry made for payment
  of deposit to Baggio Boats)

SOLUTION TO TARGET GROUP

Memorandum

To: **An Audit Manager**

From: **An Audit Senior**

Date: **14 April 2x02**

Re: **Audit of Target group**

Further to your recent request I have now undertaken a review of the various matters arising in respect of the audit of the Target Group for the year ended 31 December 2x01.

My conclusions as to the recommended accounting treatment, together with the relevant draft journal entries to adjust the financial statements, are noted in the attached schedules.

A. Senior

New Head Office Building

Using a site which the company purchased during the previous financial year, Target Holdings has constructed a new head office building. This has raised a number of accounting issues:

(i)   Which elements of cost involved in the construction and fitting out of the premises should be capitalised in the books of Target Holdings?

(ii)   How should the interest charges and arrangement fees incurred in relation to the premises be treated in the books of Target Holdings?

(iii)   What are the implications of part of the contract work on the fitting out of the premises being undertaken by a company in which one of the owner directors of Target Holdings is also involved?

(iv)   How should the disposal of the property to Fitzpatrick Properties be reflected in the financial statements of Target Holdings Limited for the year ended 31 December 2x01, and how should the subsequent lease be disclosed?

Issue 1 (i) – Calculation of Cost of New Head Office Building

In the non-current assets of Target Holdings at 31 December 2x01 the building has been capitalised at a total cost of €4,820,000 comprised as follows:

(i)   Acquisition of site €2,700,000
(ii)   Site clearance and preparation €240,000
(iii)   Construction and fitting out €1,680,000
(iv)   General administration overhead allocation capitalised €200,000.

In accordance with IAS 16, property, plant and equipment should initially be measured at its cost (IAS 16.15). Only those costs that are directly attributable to bringing the asset into working condition for its intended use should be included in its measurement (IAS 16.16). The cost of a non-current asset (whether acquired or self-constructed) comprises its purchase price and any costs directly attributable to bringing it into working condition for its intended use.

Administration and other general overhead costs, which are not directly attributable, should be excluded from the cost of a non-current asset. Therefore, the general administrative overhead of €200,000 which has been capitalised should be excluded as follows:

	DR €000	CR €000
Administrative Costs – SOCI P/L	200	
Land and Buildings		200

(Being write-off of amounts previously capitalised)

IAS 16 also sets out examples of directly attributable costs which include the following (IAS 16.17):

(i) acquisition costs (such as import duties and non-refundable purchase taxes)

(ii) the cost of site preparation

(iii) initial delivery and handling costs

(iv) installation costs

(v) professional fees (such as legal, architects' and engineers' fees).

Therefore, the legal fees and the architect's fees which were previously expensed to profit or loss should be capitalised.

The journals required are as follows:

	DR €000	CR €000
Land & Buildings	90 + 220	
Legal & Prof. Fees – SOCI P/L		90 + 220

(Being capitalisation of amounts previously written off)

This means that the adjusted cost of the land & buildings is €4,820,000 − €200,000 + €90,000 + €220,000: i.e. €4,930,000.

Issue 1 (ii) – Capitalisation of Interest

Derek Rogers has requested that we consider whether there is any opportunity to capitalise the interest charges incurred during the development phase of the property prior to occupation.

IAS 23 *Borrowing Costs* states that borrowing costs which are directly attributable to the acquisition, construction or production of a qualifying asset shall be capitalised as part of the cost of that asset (IAS 23.8). A qualifying asset is an asset that necessarily takes a substantial period of time to get ready for its intended use or sale (IAS 23.5). Clearly the head office building of Target Holdings would be classified as a qualifying asset under IAS 23.

Where the entity has borrowed specific funds for the purpose of financing the construction of a qualifying asset, eligible costs are the actual costs incurred, less any income earned on the temporary investment of such borrowings (IAS 23.12). As Target Holdings has arranged an extension to its overdraft facility, specifically to finance the construction of the Head Office Building, the actual borrowing costs incurred should be used in this instance.

Where borrowing costs are capitalised, the following rules apply in respect of commencement, suspension and cessation (IAS 23.17–23.25):

The commencement date for capitalisation is the date on which the entity first meets all of the following conditions:

(a)   expenditures are being incurred; *and*

(b)   borrowing costs are being incurred; *and*

(c)   activities that are necessary to prepare the asset for its intended use are in progress.

Capitalisation of finance costs should be suspended during periods in which active development is interrupted, and cease when substantially all the activities that are necessary to prepare the asset for its intended use or sale are complete. Therefore any capitalisation must cease when the building was occupied on 1 October 2x01.

Calculation of Interest to be Capitalised
Excluding the overhead allocation and including the legal and architects' fees, the eligible costs and the timescales involved are summarised below:

Item	Eligible borrowing period and interest rate	Interest to be capitalised
January 1 Certificate: Acquisition of Site and Legal and Architects' fees €2.89 million	1 Jan–31 March @ 9% 1 April–30 Sept @ 9.75%	€65,025 €140,888

Item	Eligible borrowing period and interest rate	Interest to be capitalised
January 31 Certificate: Architects' fees and site clearance and preparation of €300,000	1 February–31 March @ 9% 1 April–30 Sept @ 9.75%	€4,500 €14,625
31 March Certificate: Construction and fitting out of €480,000	1 April–30 Sept @ 9.75%	€23,400
Total		**€248,438**

	DR €000	CR €000
Land & Buildings	248.4	
Interest charges – SOCI P/L		248.4

(Being capitalisation of interest in respect of construction costs)

In addition, it is also appropriate to include the arrangement fees of €28,700, associated with the extension of the bank overdraft, which are an attributable cost. These fees were incurred on 1 January 2x01, and would have incurred interest charges of €2,050 ((€28.7k × 9% × 3 months) + (€28.7k × 9.75% × 6 months)). This results in a total cost of €30,750, which should be capitalised as follows:

	DR €000	CR €000
Land & Buildings	30.75	
Bank charges – SOCI P/L		30.75

(Being capitalisation of bank charges in respect of construction costs)

This brings the total adjusted cost of the building at 30 September 2x01 to €5,209,150 (i.e. €4,930k + €248.4k + €30.75k).

Depreciation
Depreciation should be charged from the time the asset is brought into use. In this case the policy is to write off land and buildings on a straight line over 50

years. Based on a cost of €5,209,150, the annual charge would be €104,183 and the monthly charge €8,682.

	DR €'000	CR €'000
Depreciation – SOCI P/L	26	
Accumulated Depreciation		26

(Being depreciation on the property for three months from 1 Oct to 31 Dec 2x01).

Disclosure

The financial statements should disclose:

(a) the amount of borrowing costs capitalised during the period; and

(b) the capitalisation rate used to determine the amount of borrowing costs eligible for capitalisation (IAS 23.26)

Issue 1 (iii) – Related Party Transaction

The construction and fitting out of the Head Office Building was undertaken by Acorn Developments Ltd, which is 40% owned by Steve Rogers, who also owns 50% of Target Holdings Limited.

Acorn and Target are not subject to joint control. In fact Steve Rogers does not appear to control either entity. Neither is there a direct shareholding interest by one company in the other. Given his equity stake, however, it is likely that Steve Rogers exercises significant influence over both companies. Acorn Developments and Target Holdings are therefore defined as related parties (IAS 24.9).

Evidence of this influence is that Target has accepted a tender significantly higher than another tender, despite the fact that all three attained the required quality threshold. This would appear to indicate that, through Steve Roger's interest in both companies, Acorn has been in a position to exert significant influence over Target.

The financial statements of Target Holdings, and the group financial statements, should disclose the following information, in accordance with IAS 24.18:

(a) a description of the relationship between the related parties (subject to significant influence);

(b) a description of the transactions (tender undertaken);

(c)   the amounts involved (amount of the tender);

(d)   any other information about the transaction, necessary for an under-standing of the potential effect of the relationship on the financial statements (e.g. other tenders at lower amount).

Issue 2 – Disposal of Building

On 31 December 2x01 Target Holdings disposed of the property to Fitzpatrick Properties Limited for €6.5m.

The first issue to be determined here is whether, in substance, the property has actually been sold to Fitzpatrick Properties Limited. In this case the risks and rewards of the asset have been transferred to the property company, and Target has no continuing rights, bar the tenancy under the lease. There is no obliga-tion or option to repurchase the property, and future increases in the value of the property will accrue to Fitzpatrick, not Target. The asset has therefore been disposed of by Target Holdings.

It follows therefore that the arrangement between Target Holdings and Fitz-patrick Properties constitutes a sale and leaseback agreement, and it should be accounted for under the rules of IAS 17 *Leases*. In accordance with IAS 17, a **finance lease** is a lease that transfers substantially all the risks and rewards of ownership of an asset to the lessee. An **operating lease** is a lease other than a finance lease (IAS 17.4).

In this case, the lease period is five years and the total amount payable under the lease will be 5 × €575,000 which is only a small part of the fair value of the leased asset. The lease is clearly therefore an operating lease.

In a sale and leaseback transaction which results in an operating lease:

(i)   any profit or loss should be recognised immediately provided it is clear that the transaction is established at fair value (IAS 17.61);

(ii)   if the sale price is above fair value, the excess should be deferred and amortised over the period for which the asset is expected to be used (IAS 17.61).

In this case, the difference between the fair value (€5.5 million) and the net book value (€5.183 million) of the recently completed Head Office Building should be taken to profit or loss during the year ended 31 December 2x01. The excess (€1 million) should be deferred and released over the period of the lease i.e. at €200,000 per annum.

The following journals will be required in respect of the disposal of the property:

	DR €'000	CR €'000
Other payables	6,500	
Disposal account		6,500
Disposal account	5,209	
Land & buildings		5,209
Accumulated depreciation	26	
Disposal account		26
Disposal account	1,317	
Deferred income (SOFP)*		1,000
Gain on disposal – SOCI P/L		317

(Being entries necessary to reflect disposal of property)

*Excess of disposal proceeds over fair value of asset. This element of the profit is deferred, and will be amortised over the period for which the asset is expected to be used (IAS 17.61).

This means that the net effect of the disposal on the Statement of Comprehensive Income is a gain of €317,000. Subject to materiality, this should be disclosed separately in accordance with IAS 1 *Presentation of Financial Statements*.

Issue 3 – Third Party Claim

Client A

In accordance with IAS 37 *Provisions, Contingent Liabilities and Contingent Assets*, a provision should be recognised when an entity has a present obligation as a result of a past event, payment is probable and a reasonable estimate can be made of the amount of the obligation (IAS 37.14).

Applying the definitions of IAS 37 to this instance:

- *present obligation* – this exists where it is more likely than not that a past event gives rise to a present obligation. Target Engineering has undertaken work during the period under review which has been found by its own expert witnesses to be defective. It appears almost certain that Target Engineering will have to make a financial settlement to compensate its customer.

- *payment is probable* – in order to settle the matter Target Engineering is likely to have to refund the €500,000 in respect of the original sale, as well as meeting the consequential losses incurred by Client A as a result of its defective work.

In the case of Target Engineering, it is likely that a present obligation exists and the recognition criteria are met. Therefore, a provision of €750,000 should be made.

The company's insurers however have indicated that they will cover part of the costs required to settle the claim. Per IAS 37, where some or all of the expenditure required to settle a provision is expected to be reimbursed by another party, the reimbursement should be recognised only when it is virtually certain that reimbursement will be received if the entity (Target Engineering) settles the obligation (IAS 37.53). In this case the Insurer has indicated in writing that it will make a settlement at up to €400,000, the limit on the insurance policy.

The following journals will be required:

	DR €'000	CR €'000
Provision – SOCI P/L	350	
Trade and other receivables	400	
Provision – SOFP		750
(Being provision in respect of Client A)		

This may also fall to be separately disclosed in accordance with IAS 1 *Presentation of Financial Statements*.

Issue 4 – Restructuring

IAS 37 *Provisions, Contingent Liabilities and Contingent Assets* permits a restructuring provision to be made when an entity has (IAS 37.72):

(a) A detailed formal plan for the restructuring, identifying at least:

   (i)   the business or part of a business concerned;

   (ii) the principal locations affected;

   (iii) the location, function, and approximate number of employees who will be compensated for terminating their services;

   (iv) the expenditures that will be undertaken;

   (v)   when the plan will be implemented; **and**

(b) has raised a valid expectation in those affected that it will carry out the restructuring by starting to implement that plan or announcing its main features to those affected by it.

In this instance, a plan was formulated during November 2x01 to withdraw from the pharmaceutical element of the business. The plan has already been discussed with and communicated to the relevant employees and their union representatives, and it is publicly known. The timetable within the plan assumes implementation commencing in February 2x02, with completion by June 2x02.

The key features of the plan are as follows:

   (i)   30 staff facing compulsory redundancy at a cost to the company of €500,000;

   (ii) 20 staff re-tasked to the Food Processing Division – training costs to convert €50,000;

   (iii) Investment in new systems to support expanded Food Processing Division €100,000.

The plan would therefore appear to fit the conditions of restructuring provisions under IAS 37. Some of the costs (i.e. the training and the system investment costs) are specifically identified by IAS 37 as not being eligible for inclusion within the restructuring provision (IAS 37.81). The provision for the balance of €500,000 should be created in the financial statements for the year ended 31 December 2x01.

A journal will be required as follows:

	DR €000	CR €000
Restructuring Provision – SOCI P/L	500	
Provision – SOFP		500
(Being provision for restructuring)		

Disclosure

An entity should disclose the following for each class of provision (IAS 37.84):

(a) the carrying amount at the beginning and end of the period

(b) additional provisions made in the period, including increases to existing provisions

(c) amounts used (i.e. incurred and charged against the provision) during the period

(d) unused amounts reversed during the period, and

(e) the increase during the period in the discounted amount arising from the passage of time and the effect of any change in the discount rate.

Impairment

In addition, Target Engineering has specialist tooling and plant and equipment which was previously utilised by the Pharmaceutical Division with a net book value of €1 million. Some of this can be redeployed to the Food Processing Division, but the remainder, which has a net book value of €250,000, can only be sold on the second-hand market for an estimated €50,000. An outline agreement to sell the equipment has already been made with a prospective buyer.

Under IAS 36 *Impairment of Assets*, all assets should be reviewed at the end of each reporting period for indications of impairment (IAS 36.9). Impairment is measured by comparing the carrying value of the asset with its recoverable amount. The recoverable amount is the higher of an asset's:

(i) fair value less costs to sell, *and*

(ii) value in use.

Fair value less costs to sell is the amount obtainable from the sale of an asset or cash-generating unit, less the costs of disposal. Value in use is the present value of the future cash flows expected to be derived from an asset or cash generating unit.

In this case, therefore, the fair value less costs to sell is the value on the second-hand market i.e. €50,000. This will be higher than the value in use, which is depressed by the fact that the division will be shortly closed down, and the equipment cannot be used in another group activity.

Journal required:

	DR €'000	CR €'000
Impairment write down of equipment – SOCI P/L	200	
Plant & equipment		200
(Being write down in respect of impairment)		

IFRS 5, *Non-Current Assets Held for Sale and Discontinued Operations*, states that a non-current asset should be classified as held for sale if its carrying amount will be recovered principally through a sale transaction (IFRS 5.6). Thus, the specialist equipment in the Pharmaceutical Division should be reclassified as follows:

	DR €'000	CR €'000
Asset held for sale	50	
Plant and equipment		50

SOLUTION TO
THE MAGNA GROUP

3 March 2x07

The Board of Directors,
Magna Holdings Group,
Riverview Drive,
Pembroke Rd,
Dublin 4

Dear Board Members,

Further to our recent meeting regarding the financial statements for the year ending 31 December 2x06, I am enclosing a report for your attention.

I will contact you shortly to arrange an appointment to discuss the matters raised in greater detail.

Yours sincerely,

Ian Cartright
Campbell Wilson & Co. Chartered Accountants

**Draft Financial Statements of the Magna Group
for the year ended 31 December 2x06**

Report Dated 3 March 2x07

Campbell Wilson & Co.

Chartered Accountants

Contents

Issue (a) Treatment of Investment in Sureguard

You have requested that we explain how the investment should be treated in the separate financial statements of Magna Holdings Limited and in the consolidated financial statements of the group.

(i) *Separate financial statements of Magna Holdings Limited*
The shares purchased in Sureguard will initially be recorded as an investment at cost. Subsequently, Magna Holdings Limited will record dividends received from Sureguard, along with any impairment in that company's value. The following entry, which has already been made by Magna Holdings Limited, accurately reflects the purchase of its shares in Sureguard Limited.

	DR €	CR €
Investment in Sureguard Ltd	140,000	
Bank		140,000

(ii) *Group financial statements*
As regards the group financial statements, there are a number of ways in which the investment could possibly be treated. I will analyse each of these in turn:

Is it a Subsidiary?
A subsidiary is an entity over which another entity (the parent) has control. Control over an investee exists when the investor is exposed to, or has rights to, variable returns and has the ability to affect those returns through its power over the investee (IFRS 10, Appendix A). In this case, although Magna holds the majority of the ordinary share capital of Sureguard, it does not have control. It must exercise control in conjunction with Standard Security Limited, and Standard Security has the power of veto over key decisions. It should therefore **not** be treated as a subsidiary.

Is it an Associate?
An associate is defined as an entity over which the investor has significant influence (IAS 28.3). In this situation, although Magna Holdings

has the opportunity to exercise significant influence, the company is managed jointly and therefore the investment should **not** be treated as an associate.

Is it a Joint Venture?

A joint venture is a joint arrangement whereby the parties that have joint control of an arrangement have rights to the net assets of the arrangement (IFRS 11, Appendix A).

Joint control exists only when decisions require the unanimous consent of the parties sharing control (IFRS 11, Appendix A).

In this case, although Magna Holdings Limited owns a majority of the shares, contractual arrangements with the other shareholder, Standard Security, mean that in practice the shareholders share control over their investee. Sureguard Limited therefore should be treated as a joint venture.

The effect of the requirement in the definition, for unanimous consent, is to give each joint venturer a veto on such decisions. This veto is what distinguishes a joint venturer from a non-controlling holder of the shares in a company, because the latter, having no veto, is subject to the policies of the majority.

In this case, therefore, despite the fact that a 70% shareholding is held by Magna Holdings Limited, the investment should be treated as a joint venture and not a subsidiary.

Accounting for Joint Ventures

In the consolidated financial statements, an investor should include a jointly controlled entity using the equity method of accounting (IFRS 11.24).

The *equity method of accounting* means that the investment is initially recognised at cost, and adjusted thereafter for the post-acquisition change in the venturer's share of the joint venture's net assets (IAS 28.3).

The following journal entry should therefore be made to record Sureguard Limited at its cost, plus a share of its post-acquisition retained profits:

	DR €	CR €
Investment in Joint Venture	140,000	
Consolidated retained earnings (€200,000 @ 70%)		140,000

Transactions between a joint venturer and a joint venture

Where a joint venturer sells assets to a joint venture, and the assets are retained by the joint venture, the joint venturer shall recognise only that portion of the gain or loss that is attributable to the interests of the other venturers (IAS 31.48).

Therefore, it will be necessary to eliminate the profit on sale of start up equipment by Magna Security (a 100% subsidiary of Magna Holdings) to Sureguard Limited as follows:

	DR €	CR €
Profit on disposal – Consolidated SOCI P/L	280,000	
Investment in Joint Venture		280,000

(Being elimination of investing group's share of profit on sale of equipment €400,000 @ 70%)

Inter-company Balances and Transactions

Because joint ventures are not part of the group, balances between the investor and its associates or joint ventures are **not** eliminated, and therefore unsettled normal trading transactions should be included as current assets or liabilities.

In this case, therefore, it is necessary to eliminate the group's share of the inter-company profit arising on the sale of equipment from Magna Security to Safeguard, but it is **not** necessary to eliminate the trading balance which exists between the two companies at the end of the year, which should remain in current assets and current liabilities.

Disclosures

Inter-company transactions

Magna Security Limited (a 100% subsidiary of Magna Holdings) and Sureguard Limited (a joint venture of Magna Holdings) are related parties, as defined by IAS 24. The sale of equipment by Magna Security to Sureguard constitutes a related party transaction.

Subject to materiality the following information should be disclosed in the financial statements of Magna Security and of the Magna Group.
- The nature of the related party relationship
- Details of the transaction (sale of equipment to Sureguard) and outstanding balances (amount due by Sureguard to the Magna Group)
- Any other information that is necessary for an understanding of the potential effect of the relationship on the financial statements (IAS 24.17).

Issue (b) Clear Scan Inc.

(i) *Computation and recognition of goodwill*
The Magna Group should recognise as an asset, goodwill acquired on its acquisition of shares in Clear Scan Inc. The goodwill should be measured as the excess of (I) over (II) below (IFRS 3.32):

(I) the aggregate of:
- the consideration transferred, measured at acquisition-date fair value;
- the amount of any non-controlling interest in the acquiree

(II) the net of the acquisition date amounts of the identifiable assets acquired and the liabilities assumed, measured in accordance with IFRS 3.

Thus, goodwill is computed as follows:

Consideration transferred	R $18m	
Translate @ 1.5		€12m
Net assets per accounts on 1 January 2x06	R $10.5m	

Amount of non-controlling interests in Clear Scan (20%)	R $2.1m	
Translate @ 1.5		€1.4m
Total		€13.4m
Identifiable net assets acquired and liabilities assumed	R $10.5m	
Translate @ 1.5		**€7m**
Goodwill (€13.4m – €7m)		**€6.4m**

IAS 36 *Impairment of Assets* requires that goodwill should, for the purpose of impairment testing, be allocated from the acquisition date to each of the acquirer's cash-generating units that is expected to benefit from the synergies of the business combination (IAS 36.80). In this instance, it is assumed that goodwill arising on the acquisition of Clear Scan is allocated in its entirety to a single cash-generating unit (i.e. Clear Scan Inc.).

A cash-generating unit to which goodwill has been allocated must be tested for impairment annually (IAS 36.90). As Clear Scan has been acquired one year ago, it will be necessary therefore to review goodwill relating to its acquisition. It would, in any event, be necessary to carry out the review, as changes in circumstances would indicate that the value of goodwill may have become impaired.

The next question to consider is whether in fact goodwill has been impaired as a result of poor trading performance, both realised and anticipated.

(ii) *Impairment review*

Impairment reviews should be performed in accordance with the requirements of IAS 36 *Impairment of Assets.*

The impairment review should comprise a comparison of the carrying amount of the goodwill, with its recoverable amount (the higher of fair value less costs to sell and value in use) (IAS 36.10). To the extent that the carrying amount exceeds the recoverable amount, goodwill is impaired and should be written down. The impairment loss should be recognised in profits or loss (IAS 36.60).

In this instance, it is assumed that the initial cost of investment of €12 million was determined, based on the projected profits of Clear

Scan over the first four years, post-takeover. These were estimated to total R$22.5 million, which converted at 1.5:1 equals €15 million (**€12 million for an 80% shareholding**).

However, based on the first year's trading, and the revised estimate of trading profits for the next three years, total profits over the four-year period are likely to be R$15 million. This would then translate to €10 million (**€8 million for an 80% shareholding**). This constitutes the value-in-use* of the cash-generating unit, and (in the absence of fair value less costs to sell) also its recoverable amount.

Consequently, the goodwill figure should be reduced by €4 million, from €6.4 million to €2.4 million.

This will require the following journal entry in the **financial statements of the Magna Holdings Group.**

	DR €'000	CR €'000
Impairment write down – SOCI P/L	4,000	
Goodwill		4,000

As the investment in Clear Scan has suffered an impairment, an adjustment will also be necessary to the **separate financial statements of Magna Holdings Limited**, as follows:

	DR €'000	CR €'000
Impairment write down – SOCI P/L	4,000	
Investment in Clear Scan Limited		4,000

This write down should be separately disclosed in both sets of financial statements, in accordance with the requirements of IAS 1 *Presentation of Financial Statements.*

Issue (c) Portable Metal Detectors – Reversal of Past Impairment

IAS 36 *Impairment of Assets* requires that an entity should assess at each reporting date whether there is any indication that an impairment loss recognised in prior

---

*It is assumed that the profits of the first four years provide an estimate of the present value of the future cash flows of Clear Scan.

periods, for an asset other than goodwill, may no longer be required or may have decreased. If any such indication exists, the entity should estimate the recoverable amount of that asset (IAS 36.110).

A reversal of an impairment loss for an asset (other than goodwill) should be recognised immediately in profit or loss, to the extent that the original impairment was charged to profit or loss. The reversal in the statement of comprehensive income is however restricted by the amount of any depreciation/amortisation that would have been charged had no impairment loss been written off in previous periods. Any remaining balance of an impairment reversal should be regarded as a revaluation (IAS 36.117–121).

IAS 36 also states that a reversal of an impairment loss for a cash-generating unit should be allocated to the assets of the unit, except for goodwill, pro rata with the carrying amounts of those assets (IAS 36.122). These increases in carrying amounts should be treated as reversals of impairment losses for individual assets, as outlined in the previous paragraph.

Events and circumstances, such as the withdrawal of a major competitor, act as triggers for an impairment review and may indicate that the recoverable amount of an asset has increased. This is the case in respect of Magna Security's equipment, whose recoverable amount appears to have increased in value as the result of a major competitor having to withdraw its products from sale.

The equipment was brought into use by Magna Security on 1 January 2x00, as part of a cash-generating unit, comprising a production line and associated tooling. Therefore, three years' depreciation had been charged at €200,000 per annum at the time of the impairment on 1 January 2x03. This resulted in a net book value of €1.4 million, which was written off in its entirety as an impairment write-down.

Subsequent depreciation which would have been charged between 1 January 2x03 and 1 October 2x06 (3 years and 9 months) amounts to €750,000. Therefore, the equipment should be reinstated at €650,000 (i.e. €1,400,000 less €750,000).

Thus, the previous impairment should be reversed as follows:

	DR €	CR €
Plant and equipment	650,000	
Reversal of impairment loss – SOCI P/L		650,000
(Being reversal of previous impairment loss)		

Depreciation expense – SOCI P/L   50,000
Accumulated depreciation   50,000
(Being depreciation for 3 months from 1 October 2x06 – 31 December 2x06

$$= \quad €650,000 \times \frac{3 \text{ months}}{39 \text{ months}})$$

Should the equipment be increased to a higher amount than €650,000, any excess will be regarded as a revaluation, and will therefore not be credited to profit or loss.

Issue (d) – Development Projects

The recognition of an item as an intangible asset requires an entity to demonstrate that the item meets (IAS 38.18):

(i) the definition of an intangible asset

(ii) the recognition criteria of IAS 38.21, which require that the expected future economic benefits that are attributable to the asset will flow to the entity, and the cost of the asset can be measured reliably.

Project A
Project A, which is development phase research, appears to meet the criteria for deferment under IAS 38.57, which requires that an entity can demonstrate all of the following:

- technical feasibility
- intention to complete the intangible asset and use or sell it
- its ability to use or sell the intangible asset
- how the intangible asset will generate future economic benefits
- the availability of adequate resources to complete and use or sell the intangible asset
- its ability to measure reliably the expenditure attributable to the intangible asset during its development.

On the assumption that Project A satisfies the foregoing conditions, Magna Medical must capitalise the expenditure relating to the development of Project A. The accounting treatment that has been adopted is correct, and no further adjustments are necessary.

Project B

During 2x06 the company commenced contract development work for another medical product company (Star Monitors Limited), developing circuitry for use in human heart monitors. Costs incurred plus an agreed mark-up profit will be paid in full by Star Monitors. Magna Medical has to date incurred €250,000 of costs on this project. Star Monitors made a payment on account of €100,000 in respect of this work in December 2x06.

The work that Magna Medical has done on behalf of Star Monitors is fully recoverable. It is therefore an asset, in the form of work in progress, and it should be included as an asset at 31 December 2x06, to the extent that Magna has not yet been reimbursed by Star Monitors.

It should be accounted for as follows:

	DR €	CR €
Work in progress – SOFP	250,000	
Capitalised development costs – SOFP		250,000
(Being research costs incurred by Magna Medical – reclassified as work in progress)		
Capitalised development costs – SOFP	100,000	
Work in progress – SOFP		100,000
(Being reclassification of costs reimbursed to Magna Medical)		

SOLUTION TO HARRINGTON MOTORS LIMITED

Memorandum

To: **Patrick Harrington**

From: **A. N. Accountant**

Subject: **Accounting Issues re Expansion**

Date: **February 2x06**

Further to our recent meeting, I have set out below my recommendations regarding the accounting treatment and disclosure of the accounting issues relating to the proposed business expansion.

Issue (a) New Dealership – Consignment Inventory

In its Conceptual Framework, the IASB outlines the circumstances when an asset should be recognised in an entity's financial statements:

> "*An asset is recognised in the statement of financial position when it is probable that the future economic benefits will flow to the entity and the asset has a cost or value that can be measured reliably* (Conceptual Framework 4.44)."

In the case of consignment inventory held by Harrington Motors the following factors are relevant in determining whether it should be recognised as an asset:

- No deposit paid to manufacturer
- Right of return without penalty
- Manufacturer bears obsolescence risk.

On this basis it appears that the risks and rewards of ownership continue to be vested in the hands of the manufacturer. No event has occurred which has had the effect of transferring commercial title to Harrington Motors. Therefore the inventory is not an asset of Harrington Motors Limited, and it should not be included in the statement of financial position until the transfer of title has crystallised. The notes to the financial statements should explain the nature of the arrangement, the amount of consignment inventory held at the year end, and the main terms under which it is held.

Journals required:

	DR €'000	CR €'000
Trade payables	170	
Purchases		170
(Being reversal of purchases in respect of goods acquired on a sale or return basis)		
Cost of sales	170	
Inventory – SOFP		170
(Being removal of goods in respect of which title has not passed to Harrington Motors)		

Issue (b) Premises

(i)   *Lease*
This type of lease is dealt with by IAS 37 *Provisions, Contingent Liabilities and Contingent Assets*, which states that:

> *"If an entity has a contract that is onerous, the present obligation under the contract shall be recognised and measured as a provision* (IAS 37.66)."

In this instance:

- Harrington Motors is committed to making payments on a leased premises, which it is not occupying, and which can not be re-let to another user
- There is a present obligation as a result of a past obligating event, i.e. the signing of a lease contract, giving rise to a legal obligation
- The transfer of economic benefits is probable

- The amount of the liability can be estimated with reasonable certainty.

Thus, the amounts payable under the lease satisfy the conditions for a provision, and the best estimate of the unavoidable lease payments should be recognised as a liability.

Journal required:

	DR €'000	CR €'000
Rental charge – SOCI P/L	720	
Provision – SOFP		720

Lease is an onerous contract

(Being provision for amounts payable under onerous lease contract)

If the effect of the time value of money is material, IAS 37 requires that the amount of a provision shall be its present value (IAS 37.45). Thus, consideration should be given to discounting the above provision to its present value.

The following details should be disclosed in the financial statements for the year ended 31 December 2x05 (IAS 37.84–85):

(I)   A brief description of the nature of the obligation, and expected timing of payment, together with an indication of any uncertainties.
(II) Details of the movement in the provision (increase of €720,000) and the closing balance (€720,000).

Subject to its materiality, the provision charged to profit or loss should also be separately disclosed, in accordance with IAS 1 *Presentation of Financial Statements*.

(ii) Costs to be capitalised in respect of new building
IAS 16 *Property, Plant & Equipment* states that, at recognition, an asset shall be measured at its cost (IAS 16.15).

IAS 16 also states that the cost of an item of property, plant and equipment comprises (IAS 16.16):

- its purchase price
- any directly attributable costs
- the initial estimate of the cost of dismantling and removing the asset.

In the case of Harrington Motors, costs amounting to €1.68 million have been capitalised in respect of the construction of a new purpose-built showroom and workshop. It may however not be appropriate to capitalise certain of these costs:

- IAS 16 provides no specific guidance as to whether site selection costs of €30,000 should be regarded as a directly attributable cost. In the absence of such guidance, IAS 8 states that management may use the most recent pronouncements of other standard-setting bodies in developing and applying an accounting policy (IAS 8.12). In this context, FRS 15 *Tangible Fixed Assets* specifically prohibits the capitalisation of site selection costs (FRS 15.9).

- Harrington Motors has also capitalised €100,000 of revenue lost during relocation as part of the premises' cost. IAS 16 excludes the *costs of opening a new facility*, and the *costs of conducting business in a new location* from being capitalised as part of an item of property, plant and equipment (IAS 16.19).

These amounts should therefore be excluded from the cost of the new premises, and the following journal entry is required:

	DR €'000	CR €'000
Lost revenue – SOCI P/L	100	
Professional costs – SOCI P/L	30	
Premises		130

(Being reversal of amounts capitalised)

Depreciation has not been charged on a correct basis by the book-keeper, who has charged two months' depreciation on the total costs capitalised in the financial statements (i.e. €1,680,000 × 2/12 × 2%) = €5,600.

The accounting policy of Harris Motors is to charge a full year's depreciation in the year of acquisition. Therefore, the correct charge is a full year's depreciation at 2%, based on the correct capitalised figure of €1,550,000, excluding land of €1,030,000. This amounts to €10,400.

Land : cost of land $ cost of legal fees re purchase of land.

Journal required:

	DR €'000	CR €'000
Depreciation expense – SOCI P/L	4.8	
Accumulated depreciation		4.8

(Being correction of depreciation charge on new premises for the year ended 31 December 2x05)

(iii) Valuation of Premises

IAS 16 states that an entity has the choice of using the cost model or the revaluation model in respect of each entire class of property, plant and equipment (IAS 16.29).

As Patrick Harrington is anxious to strengthen the statement of financial position of Harrington Motors, it seems likely that the revaluation policy will be adopted in respect of the new custom-built showroom. In this event, the premises should be carried at its fair value at the date of revaluation, less any subsequent accumulated depreciation and subsequent impairment losses (IAS 16.31).

IAS 16 defines fair value as . . . *the amount for which an asset could be exchanged between knowledgeable, willing parties in an arm's length transaction* (IAS 16.6). Applying this definition to Harrington Motors, the current market value of €1.9 million would be the appropriate valuation of the premises.

Journal required:

	DR €'000	CR €'000
Accumulated depreciation	10.4	
Premises		10.4

(Being elimination of accumulated depreciation at the time of revaluation)

	DR €'000	CR €'000
Premises	360.4	
Revaluation surplus – SOCI OCI		360.4

(Being revaluation of premises to fair value)

350 reval
10.4 Acc D

The following information should be disclosed where assets are stated at revalued amounts (IAS 16.77):

- Effective date of valuation;
- Whether an independent valuer was involved;
- Methods and assumptions applied in estimating fair value;
- Extent to which fair value was determined with reference to observable prices in an active market, or using other valuation techniques;
- The carrying amount that would have been recognised under the cost model;
- The revaluation surplus, indicating the change for the period, and any restrictions on the distribution of the balance to shareholders.

Lecture note: The question states that the tax implications of adjustments should be ignored. If this were not the case, Harrington Motors would be required to provide for deferred tax in respect of the revaluation surplus, in accordance with IAS 12 *Income Taxes*.

Deferred Tax liability

Issue (c) – New Equipment

IAS 16 states that the costs of testing whether an asset is functioning properly should be regarded as directly attributable costs (IAS 16.17).

Additionally, IAS 16 states that costs incurred, while an item capable of operating in the manner intended by management has yet to be brought into use (or is operated at less than full capacity), should be expensed (IAS 16.20).

Applying these requirements to the new equipment of Harrington Motors:

- The various essential costs (totalling €25,000) incurred during the commissioning period should be capitalised.
- Costs of €45,000 were incurred during the initial operating period, as due to slack demand the equipment was used only intermittently. These costs must be expensed, in accordance with IAS 16, and cannot be capitalised as part of the cost of the equipment.

Journal required:

	DR €'000	CR €'000
Plant & equipment	25	
Expenses – SOCI P/L		25

(Being the capitalisation of essential commissioning costs, which had been expensed to profit or loss)

Issue (d) – New Customer

The lease of cars to the local firm over three years constitutes an operating lease, as defined by IAS 17, *Leases* (IAS 17.4). This standard requires that any asset held for use in operating leases by a lessor should be carried in the statement of financial position of the lessor (IAS 17.49). In this case, the cars should be recorded as a non-current asset by Harrington Motors.

In accordance with IAS 17, the depreciation policy for leased assets should be consistent with the lessor's normal depreciation policy for similar assets, and depreciation should be calculated in accordance with IAS 16 (IAS 17.53). As the cars are expected to be traded in every three years by Harrington Motors, they should be depreciated over this period net of their expected residual value.

In the case of an operating lease, no selling profit should be recognised by a dealer lessor (such as Harrington Motors), as the transaction is not the equivalent of a sale (IAS 17.55).

IAS 17 states that *rental income* receivable by a lessor from an operating lease should normally be recognised as income on a straight-line basis over the lease period (IAS 17.50). In the case of Harrington Motors, however, it will be appropriate to recognise income in accordance with the payment schedule (€200k in year 1, €100k in year 2, and €75k in year 3). This treatment is justified where … *another systematic basis is more representative of the time pattern in which use benefit derived from the leased asset is diminished* (IAS 17.50). In the case of car rental, it can be assumed that the quality of use from the asset diminishes in line with age. Alternatively, the rental income could be recognised on a straight line basis.

The following information should be disclosed in accordance with IAS 16.73 and IAS 17.35:

- Measurement basis used for determining the gross carrying amount;
- Depreciation methods used;
- The gross carrying amount and the accumulated depreciation at the beginning and end of the period;
- Future minimum lease payments under non-cancellable operating leases – not later than one year, between one and five years and over five years;
- General description of leasing arrangements.

Issue (e) – Potential Acquisition

(1)   Separate Financial Statements of Harrington Motors Limited

(i)   Outright purchase of 100% of the share capital of Focus Ltd

The investment in Focus Limited will be shown either at *cost* or in accordance with *IFRS 9* (IAS 27.10). In accordance with company policy, the former basis will apply, and the following journal entry would be required:

	DR €'000	CR €'000
Investment in Focus Ltd	4,000	
Bank		1,000
Share Capital		500
Share Premium		2,500
(Being purchase of 100% of shares in Focus Limited)		

(ii)   Purchase of an 18% stake in Focus Limited

An associate is defined as an entity over which the investor has significant influence (IAS 28.3).

Significant influence is defined as the power to participate in the financial and operating policy decisions of the investee, but is not control or joint control of these policies (IAS 28.3). If an investor holds 20% or more of the voting power of the investee, it is presumed that the investor has significant influence, unless it can be clearly demonstrated that this is not the case. Conversely, if the investor holds less than 20% of the voting power, it is presumed that the investor does not have significant influence, unless such influence can be clearly demonstrated (IAS 28.5).

IAS 28 identifies representation on the board of directors as providing evidence of significant influence (IAS 28.6). Thus, although only 18% of the shares in Focus Limited are held by Harrington Motors, it is probable that significant influence is still exercised through board representation.

An investment in an associate shall be accounted for in an investor's separate financial statements either at cost or in accordance with

IFRS 9 (IAS 27.10). On the assumption that the former basis will apply, the following journal entry would be required:

	DR €'000	CR €'000
Investment in Focus Limited	850	
Bank		850
(Being purchase of 18% of Focus Limited)		

(2) Consolidated Financial Statements

(a) Accounting treatment

- **100% purchase – subsidiary**
  IFRS 10 *Consolidated Financial Statements* defines a subsidiary as an entity that is controlled by another entity (IFRS 10, Appendix A). Focus Limited will be a subsidiary undertaking of Harrington Motors Limited, and IFRS 3 stipulates the following requirements in relation to the preparation of consolidated financial statements:

  (i) all business combinations to be accounted for by the acquisition method (IFRS 3.4)

  (ii) the consideration transferred should be measured at fair value, which should be calculated as the sum of the acquisition-date fair values of the assets transferred by the acquirer, the liabilities incurred by the acquirer to the former owners of the acquiree and the equity interests issued by the acquirer (IFRS 3.37).

  (iii) the acquirer shall measure the identifiable assets acquired and the liabilities assumed at their acquisition date fair values (IFRS 3.18).

  (iv) The acquirer shall recognise goodwill as (ii) above + the amount of any non-controlling interest in the acquiree less (iii) above (IFRS 3.32).

  The following consolidation adjustments will be necessary, when incorporating Focus Limited into the consolidated financial statements:

	DR €	**CR** €
Individual Assets/Liabilities	3,196,192*	
Goodwill	803,808	
Investment in Focus Limited		4,000,000

*(Non-current assets €2,867,198** + Current assets €1,482,615)
– (Current liabilities €978,121 + L. T. liabilities €175,500)
**Including revaluation of property

- **18% purchase – associate**

  In the consolidated financial statements, IAS 28 *Investments in Associates and Joint Ventures* requires that all associates be accounted for using the equity method.

  The cost of investing in Focus Limited will already have been recorded in the separate financial statements of Harrington Motors at 30 June 2x06. No further adjustment will be necessary, at that date, in order to incorporate Focus Limited into the consolidated financial statements.

- **Subsequent profits**

  For a 100% purchase

  - The profit/loss of Focus Limited arising between 1 July 2x06 and 31 December 2x06 will be included under the relevant headings in the Statement of Comprehensive Income of the Group.
  - Inter-company trading should be eliminated.

  For an 18% purchase

  - The profit or loss of the Harrington Motors Group will include the group's share of the profit or loss of Focus Limited from 1 July 2x06.

SOLUTION TO
THE O'NEILL GROUP

Grimbsy, Holt & Co.

Accounting Issues relating to the 2x05 Financial Statements of the O'Neill Group of Companies

Report dated 16 February 2x06

Contents

Mr David O'Neill,
Managing Director,
The O'Neill Group,
Central Road,
Ballindown

16 February 2x06

Report on accounting issues in respect of 2x05 Financial Statements

Dear Mr O'Neill,

Further to our recent discussions, we enclose a copy of our report which sets out the appropriate accounting treatment and disclosure requirements regarding various matters which have arisen in respect of the 2x05 Financial Statements of the O'Neill Group.

I look forward to discussing these issues with you in detail when we meet next week.

Yours sincerely

A. N. Accountant
Grimbsy, Holt & Co.

Issue 1 – O'Neill Retail Ltd

Example four of Appendix B of IAS 37 *Provisions, Contingent Liabilities and Contingent Assets* clearly sets out the correct accounting treatment in respect of the new refunds policy.

(a) *There is a present obligation as a result of a past obligating event*
The obligating event is the sale of the product giving rise to a constructive obligation, because the policy of the store has created a valid expectation on the part of customers that the store will refund purchases.

(b) *There is a probable transfer of economic benefit*

Conclusion – A provision is required for the best estimate of the cost of refunds. It is assumed that the goods which are returned can be resold. Therefore the following provision is required:

$$€550,000 * 0.2 * .05 = €5,500$$

	DR €	CR €
Cost of sales	5,500	
Provision – SOFP		5,500

Disclosures required
For each class of provision (IAS 37.84):

- the carrying amount at the beginning and end of the period;
- additional provisions made in the period, including increases to existing provisions;
- amounts used during the period;
- unused amounts reversed during the period; and
- the increase during the period in the discounted amount arising from the passage of time, and the effect of any change in the discount rate.

Comparative information is *not* required.

The following information should also be disclosed for each class of provision (IAS 37.85):

- a brief description of the nature of the obligation and the expected timing of any resulting outflows of economic benefits;

- an indication of the uncertainties about the timing or amount of any outflows including the major assumptions adopted;
- the amount of any expected reimbursement, stating the amount of any asset recognised for that expected reimbursement.

Issue 2 – Sale of O'Neill Restaurant Ltd

(a) *Treatment in Parent Company's Separate Financial Statements*
The cash received on disposal of the investment and the gain on that disposal will be recorded in the parent company's separate financial statements. The gain will be the difference between the consideration received and the carrying value of the investment.

	€
Disposal proceeds	175,000
Cost of investment	(3,000)
Profit on disposal	172,000

The following journal entry is required in respect of the disposal:

| | DR | CR |
	€	€
Cash/Bank	175,000	
Investment at cost		3,000
Profit on disposal – SOCI P/L		172,000

Given its materiality, the profit on disposal should be separately disclosed, in accordance with IAS 1 *Presentation of Financial Statements*.

(b) *Treatment in Group Financial Statements*
If a parent loses control over a subsidiary, in accordance with IFRS 10, it should:

- derecognise the assets and liabilities of the former subsidiary
- recognise any investment retained in the former subsidiary at its fair value at the date when control is lost
- recognise the gain or loss associated with the loss of control (IFRS 10.25).

O'Neill Restaurant will cease to be consolidated as a subsidiary of the O'Neill Group on 31 December 2x05, and its income and expenses are included in the consolidated financial statements until that date (IFRS 10.20). At that date, by virtue of O'Neill Enterprises being able to exercise significant influence over O'Neill Restaurant, it will become an associate of the Group (IAS 28.3).

The following journal entry will be required in the group financial statements in respect of the disposal, and the reclassification of O'Neill Restaurant as an associate:

	DR €	CR €
Bank	175,000	
Non-controlling Int.* (€156,000 × 40%)	62,400	
Investment in Associate**	154,000	
Net assets		156,000
Profit on disposal – SOCI P/L		235,400

   *Non-controlling Interest: (Net assets of O'Neill Restaurant @ 31/12/2x05 × 40%)

   **Investment in Associate (Fair value of retained 30% interest on date of disposal as given in question)

Presentation and Disclosure

- O'Neill Restaurant was a subsidiary of the O'Neill Group up to 31 December 2x05. Its operations and cash flows were clearly distinguishable from the rest of the group, and it was therefore a component of the group, in accordance with IFRS 5 *Non-current assets held for sale and discontinued operations* (IFRS 5 Appendix A).

- A discontinued operation is a component of an entity that meets the conditions outlined in paragraph 32 of IFRS 5. For a component to be classified as a discontinued operation, it must be held for sale, or already disposed of, and meet one of the following criteria:

- It must represent a major line of business or geographical area of operations
- It must be part of a single co-ordinated plan to dispose of a separate major line of business or geographical area of operations
- It must be a subsidiary acquired exclusively with a view to resale.

As O'Neill Restaurant was a major line of business in the O'Neill Group, the disposal of a controlling interest in that company constitutes a discontinued operation, in accordance with IFRS 5.

Disclosures required

(i)   In the statement of comprehensive income:
A single amount, being the total of the after tax profit or loss of the discontinued operation, and the after tax gain or loss from disposing of the assets comprising the discontinued operation (IFRS 5.33). This disclosure is also required for prior periods presented in the financial statements (IFRS 5.34).

(ii) In the notes or on the face of the statement of comprehensive income (IFRS 5.33):

- The revenue, expenses and pre-tax profit or loss and the income tax expense of the discontinued operation
- The gain or loss on disposal of the subsidiary
- The net cash flows attributable to the operating, investing and financing activities of the subsidiary.

This disclosure is also required for prior periods presented in the financial statements (IFRS 5.34).

(iii) Additional disclosures in the notes for assets that have been sold in the current period (IFRS 5.41):

- A description of the non-current asset
- A description of the facts and circumstances of the sale
- The gain or loss recognised and, if not separately presented on the face of the statement of comprehensive income, the caption in the comprehensive income statement that includes that gain or loss.

(c) Treatment in 2x06 Consolidated Financial Statements

As and from 31 December 2x05, O'Neill Restaurant meets the definition of an Associate under IAS 28 *Investment in Associates and Joint Ventures,* on the basis that the O'Neill Group exercises significant influence and O'Neill Restaurant is neither a subsidiary nor a joint venture of the group (IAS 28.3).

In accordance with IAS 28, O'Neill Restaurant should be accounted for in the consolidated financial statements of the O'Neill Group in 2x06, using the equity method (IAS 28.16). The investment should initially be recognised at cost (in this case, the fair value at 31 December 2x05 represents deemed cost), and adjusted thereafter for the investor's share of the post-acquisition change in the investee's net assets.

The profit or loss of the investor should include the investor's share of the profit or loss of the investee (IAS 28.3). Investments in associates should be classified as a non-current asset (IAS 28.15).

Issue 3 – Potential Acquisition of Reid Enterprises Ltd

(a)   Accounting Policies

Valuation of Property
IAS 16 *Property, Plant and Equipment* requires that an entity should apply either the cost model or the revaluation model to an entire class of property, plant and equipment (IAS 16.29).

Reid Enterprises applies the revaluation model in respects of its premises. Where the revaluation model is chosen, IAS 16 requires that assets be carried at their fair value at the date of the revaluation, less any subsequent accumulated depreciation and subsequent impairment losses (IAS 16.31).

Deferred Tax
IAS 12 *Income Taxes* requires that full provision be made for almost all temporary differences. Thus, in providing for deferred tax in respect of the temporary difference arising on the revaluation of its premises, Reid Enterprises is fully in compliance with IAS 12. Although no agreement has been entered into for the sale of the premises, it is still necessary to provide for deferred tax on the revaluation of the building. Further, IAS 12 does not permit deferred tax provisions to be discounted.

Related Parties
IAS 24 *Related Party Disclosures* does not require the disclosure of the names of related parties. Thus, Reid Enterprises is not required to disclose the names of related companies with whom transactions have taken place. The nature of the related party relationship must, however, be disclosed.

(b) Goodwill arising on the purchase of Reid Enterprises

	€
Consideration	2,000,000
Net assets at fair value*	(849,850)
Goodwill	1,150,150

*As the non-current assets of Reid Enterprises are at market value, and as a deferred tax provision has been made in respect of the revalued premises, no further fair value adjustments are required.

(c)   *Journal entry required to incorporate the trade and assets of Reid Enterprises Ltd into the books at 1 January 2x06*

	DR €	CR €
Goodwill	1,150,150	
Non-current assets	2,100,000	
Current assets	2,350,000	
Current liabilities		2,100,150
Long-term liabilities		1,100,000
Provisions		400,000
Bank		2,000,000

The acquisition of Reid Enterprises will require disclosure as a non-adjusting event after the reporting period, in accordance with IAS 10 *Events after the Reporting Period*. Disclosure of the nature of the event will be required, as well as an estimate of the financial effect (IAS 10.21).

SOLUTION TO FITZWILLIAM GROUP

(a) Fitzwilliam Construction Ltd

Construction Contract under IAS 11

Accounting treatment

The ultimate outcome of the contract should be estimated as follows:

	€'000	€'000
Contract price		1,700
Less:		
Costs to date	920	
Completion costs	850	
Provision for clean up	200	1,970
Estimated loss		270

This expected loss must be recognised in full.

As the construction work is well underway, the outcome of the contract can be estimated reliably. Therefore the contract revenue to date should be recognised on a percentage of completion basis (IAS 11.22). This can be measured on the basis of costs to date and costs to completion. The revenue to date is therefore:

$$1,700,000 \times \frac{920,000}{1,770,000} = €883,616$$

Costs to date amount to €920,000.

The contract account is shown below:

Contract Account

Bank/creditors	920,000	Cost of sales (note 1)	1,153,616
Provision for clean up	200,000	Balance c/f	850,000
Revenue	883,616		
	2,003,616		2,003,616

Note 1
In a loss-making contract, the cost of sales will equal revenue + the loss to be recognised. In this case, cost of sales = 1,153,616 (i.e. 883,616 + 270,000).

Extract from Financial Statements

Statement of Comprehensive Income for the year ended 31/12/2x05

	€
Revenue	883,616
Cost of sales	(1,153,616)
Gross loss	270,000

Statement of Financial Position as at 31/12/2x05

	€
Current assets	
Amount recoverable on contract	850,000
Current liabilities	
Bank overdraft	920,000
Provision for clean up	200,000
Net liabilities	270,000
Equity	
Accumulated loss	270,000

Journals:

	DR €	CR €
Contract a/c	920,000	
Bank/Creditors		920,000
(Being costs to date on contract)		
Cost of sales – SOCI P/L	1,153,616	
Contract a/c		1,153,616
(Being costs to date transferred to cost of sales)		
Contract a/c	883,616	
Revenue – SOCI P/L		883,616
(Being revenue recognised on contract)		

Provision

IAS 37 states that a provision should be recognised when (IAS 37.14):

- An entity has a present obligation (legal or constructive) as a result of a past event;
- *It is probable that an outflow of resources will be required to settle the obligation; and*
- A reliable estimate can be made of the amount of the obligation.

In the case of Fitzwilliam Construction, there is a constructive obligation (giving rise to a valid expectation on the part of those affected by it) that the entity will clear up contamination, together with the probable transfer of economic benefits, so a provision of €200,000 is required.

	DR €	CR €
Contract a/c – SOCI P/L	200,000	
Provision – SOFP		200,000

The following disclosures are required (IAS 37.84):

- Amount of the provision at the beginning and end of the period
- Additional provisions made in the period

- A brief description of the nature of the obligation and the expected timing of any resulting outflows of economic benefits
- An indication of the uncertainties about the amount or timing of outflows

Additional disclosures required
The disclosures required in respect of construction contracts are outlined in IAS 11.39–45:

- Amount of contract revenue recognised as revenue in the period
- Method for determining revenue
- Method for determining stage of completion
- Gross amount due from customers
- Aggregate of costs incurred, recognised losses and retentions
- Advances received
- Amount of retentions

(b) Fitzwilliam Rental Ltd

(i)   Year ended 31 December 2x05

Docklands Property
The disused building was purchased at a cost of €1.5 million on 1 January 2x05. At that time the intention was to develop the property and subsequently to let it to professional firms. IAS 40 defines investment property as "… property … held to earn rentals or for capital appreciation or both" (IAS 40.5).

At the time of its purchase, the building purchased by Fitzwilliam Rental therefore qualifies as investment property under IAS 40. The acquisition cost of €1.5 million + the renovation cost of €300,000 will be included as investment property in the statement of financial position.

On the 31 December 2x05 the property will be carried at fair value of €2 million, in accordance with the accounting policy of Fitzwilliam

Rental. The gain of €200,000 will be recognised in profit or loss for the year ended 31 December 2x05 (IAS 40.35).

	DR €	CR €
Investment property	200,000	
Gain on revaluation of investment property – SOCI P/L		200,000

If it is considered material, the work carried out by Fitzwilliam Construction Ltd should be disclosed as a related party transaction under IAS 24 *Related Party Disclosures*. The following disclosures will be required by IAS 24.17:

- The nature of the related party relationship (parties subject to common control by Fitzwilliam Group Ltd)
- Information about the transaction (€200,000 work done by Fitzwilliam Construction Ltd)
- Details of outstanding balances

(ii) Year ending 31 December 2x06

Docklands Property
In February 2x06, the docklands property was valued at €2.1 million, and the group decided to relocate its headquarters to this building. Owner-occupied property is excluded from being treated as investment property (IAS 40.9). Thus, the docklands property is reclassified at that date, and will then be dealt with under the rules of IAS 16.

At the time of commencement of owner-occupation, the fair value at the date of change of use is deemed to be the 'cost' of the property under its new classification (IAS 40.60). The increase in value of €100,000 (€2.1 million – €2 million) up to the date of transfer should be recorded in profit for the period.

	DR €	CR €
Investment property	100,000	
Gain on revaluation of investment property – SOCI P/L		100,000
PPE	2,100,000	
Investment property		2,100,000

Disclosures

- The fact that Fitzwilliam Rental uses the revaluation model for investment property (IAS 40.75)
- Amounts recognised in profit or loss (IAS 40.75)

Old Group Headquarters
In February 2x06, Fitzwilliam Rental managed to secure new tenants for this property. The old headquarters therefore become investment property at this date. This represents a transfer from owner occupation to investment property, and the old headquarters will now be dealt with under IAS 40.

IAS 16 should be applied up to the date of reclassification. Any difference arising between the carrying amount under IAS 16 at that date, and the fair value, is accounted for as a revaluation under IAS 16 (IAS 40.61).

The book value of the property was €1.5 million, and the market value at the date of letting in February 2x06 was €1.8 million. Thus, the increase of €300,000 is recorded as a revaluation surplus prior to reclassification, and it is **not** included in profit or loss.

	DR €	CR €
PPE	300,000	
Revaluation surplus – SOCI OCI		300,000
Investment property	1,800,000	
PPE		1,800,000

(iii) Air conditioning and heating system

IAS 16.13 states that parts of some property, plant and equipment may require replacement at regular intervals. Such parts will be included in property, plant and equipment when the cost is incurred, if the recognition criteria of the standard are met. The standard also requires that each significant part of an item of property, plant and equipment should be depreciated separately.

Thus, the building and air conditioning system are treated as separate assets and depreciated over their respective useful lives:

The depreciation of the building for the year ending 31 December 2x06 will be €1,900,000 × 10/12 × 1/50 = €31,667.

The depreciation of the heating system for the year ending 31 December 2x06 will be €200,000 × 10/12 × 1/10 = €16,667.

(c) Fitzwilliam Retail Ltd

In March 2x05, Fitzwilliam Retail sold one of its department stores to a third party, and entered into a 10-year operating lease to lease back the store at a market rental.

IAS 17 *Leases* states that, if it is clear that the transaction is carried out at fair value, the profit or loss should be recognised immediately (IAS 17.61).

The following journal will be required:

	DR €	CR €
Bank	2,500,000	
Property, plant and equipment		2,200,000
Profit on disposal – SOCI P/L		300,000
(Being disposal of property)		

(d) Fitzwilliam Group

(i) Proposed dividend

On 14 January 2x06 the Board of Fitzwilliam Group Ltd proposed a dividend of €750,000 in respect of the year ended 31 December

2x05. IAS 10, *Events after the Reporting Period,* states that dividends declared after the reporting period shall not be recognised as a liability at the end of the reporting period (IAS 10.12). Such dividends are disclosed in the notes in accordance with IAS 1 *Presentation of Financial Statements.*

(ii)   *Share options*

The Board of Fitzwilliam Group Ltd agreed to grant 50 share options to each of its 100 employees with a commencement date of 1 January 2x06. This agreement is defined as an equity settled share-based payment under IFRS 2 *Share-Based Payment.*

IFRS 2 requires that, as the services received from the employees do not qualify as an asset, they should be recognised as expenses (IFRS 2.8). It also requires that the charge should be measured at the fair value of the shares or share options at the date of grant of the options (IFRS 2.11). IFRS 2 further requires that the expense be recognised over the vesting period (IFRS 2.15).

The total of the fair value of share options granted equals:
$50 \times 100 \times 20 = €100,000$.

It is likely that 25% of employees will leave during the four-year vesting period, and will therefore forfeit their rights under the share option scheme.

The total cost of the scheme is therefore likely to be €75,000 (i.e. €100,000 × .75). This will be expensed over the four-year vesting period, giving rise to an annual charge in the statement of comprehensive income of €18,750.

The following journal will be required:

	DR €	CR €
Share option expense – SOCI P/L	18,750	
Equity reserve – SOFP		18,750
(In each of years 1–4)		

Disclosure requirements

IFRS 2 requires that the following information be disclosed (IFRS 2.44–50):

- Information that enables users of financial statements to understand the nature and extent of share-based payment arrangements
- Information that enables users to understand how fair value was determined
- Information that enables users to understand the effect of share-based transactions on the entity's profit or loss for the period and on its financial position.

SOLUTION TO HARDING GROUP

Memorandum

From: B. Inline

To: **Group Financial Director, Harding plc**

Date: **1 March 2x07**

Further to our recent meeting, I have detailed below my views in respect of accounting issues arising in respect of the financial statements for the year ended 31 December 2x06.

(a) Disposal of Golf plc

(i)   *Costs included in 'Other Operating Expenses'*

Operating costs incurred

The IASB's *Conceptual Framework* states that "…the definition of expenses encompasses losses as well as those expenses that arise in the course of the ordinary activities of the entity" (Paragraph 4.33).

Operating costs incurred of €92 million appear to comply with the above definition and they are therefore correctly included as an expense in Golf's Statement of Comprehensive Income for the year ended 31 December 2x06.

Provision for future operating losses

IAS 37 *Provisions, Contingent Liabilities and Contingent Assets* states that "provisions shall not be recognised for future operating losses" (IAS 37.63). The inclusion of a provision for future operating losses of €30 million in the Statement of Comprehensive Income of Golf is therefore in breach of the rules of IAS 37. Such losses should instead be charged to expense as incurred.

Impairment of assets

IAS 36 *Impairment of Assets* requires that an entity shall assess at each reporting date whether there is any indication that an asset may be impaired. If any such indication exists, the entity shall estimate the recoverable amount of the asset (IAS 36.9).

IAS 36 requires that, if the recoverable amount of an asset is less than its carrying amount, the carrying amount of the asset shall be reduced to its recoverable amount (IAS 36.59). Should an impairment loss arise, it should be recognised immediately in profit or loss (IAS 36.60).

Thus, the inclusion by Golf of an impairment loss of €18 million in its Statement of Comprehensive Income is in line with the requirements of IAS 36.

(ii) *Accounting treatment of Golf in the consolidated financial statements*
Golf plc has been a loss-making subsidiary for several years, and the Board of Harding plc agreed at a Board meeting in November 2x06 to sell Golf to a third party as a going concern. The Group Financial Director is keen to exclude Golf from the consolidated financial statements as it is no longer part of continuing group operations.

IFRS 10 *Consolidated Financial Statements*, however, requires that consolidation of an investee should cease only when an investor loses control of an investee (IFRS 10.20).

Thus, Golf should continue to be consolidated as part of the Harding Group in the 2x06 financial statements. As it has already been consolidated, Golf cannot be classified as a disposal group held for sale.

The question also arises as to whether Golf should be classified as a discontinued operation in the 2x06 consolidated financial statements. A discontinued operation is defined as a component of an entity that either has been disposed of or is classified as held for sale (IFRS 5, Appendix A). As Golf fails to satisfy either condition at 31 December 2x06, it should not be treated as a discontinued operation in the 2x06 consolidated financial statements.

(b) Harding plc properties

(i) *Head office property*
The treatment of Harding's head office property is determined by IAS 16 *Property, Plant and Equipment.*

Harding has opted to apply the revaluation model as the company's accounting policy, as permitted by IAS 16 (IAS 16.29). If an asset's carrying amount is increased as a result of a revaluation, the increase shall be credited to other comprehensive income and accumulated in equity under the heading of revaluation surplus (IAS 16.39). Where an asset's carrying amount is decreased as a result of a revaluation, the decrease shall be recognised in other comprehensive income to the extent of any credit balance existing in the revaluation surplus in respect of that asset (IAS 16.40).

At 31 December 2x05, Harding revalued its head office property from €20 million to €31 million. The property has later fallen in value to €29 million at 31 December 2x06. As there is a revaluation surplus of €11 million at 31 December 2x05, the decrease in value a year later will be set against the revaluation surplus on the same property.

The following journal entry will be required:

	DR €'m	CR €'m
Revaluation surplus – SOCI OCI	2	
Property, Plant & Equipment		2
(Being decrease in value of head office property at 31 December 2x06)		

(ii)   Investment property

IAS 40 permits an entity to choose as its accounting policy either the fair value model or the cost model (IAS 40.30). Harding plc owns one investment property, which was purchased during 2x05, and included in the financial statements at 31 December 2x05 using the cost model.

The Board wishes to employ the fair value model in respect of investment property at 31 December 2x06. This represents a change in measurement basis, and it is therefore a change in accounting policy, as defined by IAS 8 *Accounting Policies, Changes in Accounting Estimates and Errors* (IAS 8.5).

IAS 8 states that an entity is permitted to change an accounting policy only if the change:

- is required by an IFRS *or*
- results in the financial statements providing reliable and more relevant information about the effects of transactions, other events or conditions on the entity's financial position, financial performance or cash flows (IAS 8.14).

In respect of Harding plc's decision to adopt the fair value model for its investment property, this is *not* required by an IFRS. Thus, if the shift to the fair value model is to be permissible, under IAS 8, it must result in the financial statements providing reliable and more relevant information. On the assumption that this is the case, Harding would be allowed to change its accounting policy, and to adopt the fair value model in respect of its investment property.

IAS 8 states that, when an entity changes an accounting standard voluntarily, it shall apply the change retrospectively (IAS 8.19(b)). Paragraph 23 of IAS 8 reiterates the need for retrospective application, except where it is impracticable to determine either the period-specific effects or the cumulative effect of the change.

In the case of Harding plc, therefore, the value of its investment property should be amended retrospectively at 31 December 2x05, if it is practicable to make this adjustment. If not, the increase in value should be effected entirely in the 2x06 financial statements.

On the assumption that retrospective adjustment is not practicable, the increase in value of €4 million should be recognised in profit or loss in the 2x06 financial statements (IAS 40.35). The following journal entry will be required:

	DR €'m	CR €'m
Investment property	4	
Revaluation gain – SOCI P/L		4
(Being gain on revaluation of investment property at 31 December 2x06)		

(c) Holly plc

(i) Final net asset valuation of Holly

IFRS 3 *Business Combinations* recognises that it is not always possible to accurately determine the value of some assets at the date of acquisition. In these circumstances, IFRS 3 states that provisional values should be used in an entity's financial statements during the measurement period for the items for which the accounting is incomplete (IFRS 3.45). However the measurement period shall not exceed one year from the acquisition date (IFRS 3.45).

In respect of the acquisition of Holly plc on 1 March 2x05, goodwill was provisionally computed, based on a net asset value of €8 million. The final valuation, which became available in December 2x06, shows a net asset value of €7 million. As this information was not available within 12 months of the acquisition date, no adjustment to the provisional value is permitted under IFRS 3. An exception to this rule is only permissible in order to correct an error, in accordance with IAS 8 *Accounting Policies, Changes in Accounting Estimates and Errors (IFRS 3.50)*.

[handwritten margin note: Macn 06 = 12 uona]

If the adjustment of €1 m relates to the correction of a material prior period error, accounting for the business combination will be amended as follows;

	DR	CR
Goodwill	€1m	
Net assets		€1m

Otherwise, the €1m should be charged to profit or loss for the year ended 31 December 2x06:

	DR	**CR**
Impairment loss – SOCI P/L	€1m	
Net assets		€1m

(ii) *Development costs*

IAS 38 *Intangible Assets* distinguishes between the research phase and the development phase of work carried out by an entity (IAS 38.52).

Research phase

In the research phase of an internal project, an entity cannot demonstrate that an intangible asset exists that will generate probable future economic benefits (IAS 38.54). The Standard states that no intangible asset arising from research shall be recognised (IAS 38.54). It goes on to require that expenditure on research should be recognised as an expense as it is incurred (IAS 38.54).

The research carried out by Holly plc in 2x05 was written off, as management was not sufficiently confident of the ultimate profitability of the project. This treatment was correct, as the project at that stage would have been regarded as being in a research phase.

IAS 38 states that expenditure on an intangible item that was initially recognised as an expense shall not be recognised as part of the cost of an intangible asset at a later date (IAS 38.71). Thus, the expenditure incurred by Holly in 2x05 cannot be capitalised in 2x06, even though the project may have entered a development phase by that time.

Development phase

IAS 38 sets out the criteria which must be satisfied if an intangible asset arising from the development phase of an internal project is to be recognised. An entity must be able to demonstrate all of the following (IAS 38.57):

- Technical feasibility
- Intention to complete the intangible asset and use or sell it
- Ability to use or sell the asset
- How the intangible asset will generate probable future economic benefits

- Availability of adequate technical, financial and other resources to complete the project
- Ability to measure reliably the expenditure attributable to the intangible asset during its development.

Holly plc's research project to develop a new chemical appears to have entered a development phase in 2x06. Production is expected to commence in the next few months, trading profits from sales are estimated at €20 million, and the Board has decided to complete the project.

Thus, the expenditure incurred during 2x06, amounting to €10 million, should be capitalised as an intangible asset at 31 December 2x06.

(d) Deferred tax issues relating to Prospect plc

IAS 12 *Income Taxes* requires that a deferred tax liability be recognised for most taxable temporary differences (IAS 12.15).

The following issues arise in respect of the deferred tax position of Prospect plc, which is an acquisition target of the Harding Group:

(i)   *Gains on readily marketable investments*
Prospect plc has made a gain of €5 million in respect of its investments, which has been recorded as income in its financial statements. This gain will be taxed only on disposal of the investments. Thus, there is a taxable temporary difference of €5 million, as future taxable profit will exceed future accounting profit.

As the corporation tax rate is 30%, this will give rise to a deferred tax liability of €1.5 million. This should be charged to profit or loss.

(ii) *Accrual for pension contributions*
Prospect plc intends making an additional accrual for pension costs of €1 million, which will not be allowable for tax purposes until it is paid. This is a deductible temporary difference, as Prospect's future taxable profit will be less than its future accounting profit.

As the corporation tax rate is 30%, this will reduce Prospect's deferred tax liability by €300,000. This gain will also be included in profit or loss.

The net effect of these two temporary differences is an increase in the deferred tax provision of €1.2 million. Thus, a journal entry is required as follows:

	DR €'000	CR €'000
Deferred tax charge – SOCI P/L	1,200	
Deferred tax provision – SOFP		1,200

SOLUTION TO DARCY GROUP

Memorandum

To: Mr Fitzwilliam

Subject: Various Accounting Issues relating to the 2x07 Financial Statements of the Darcy Group of Companies

Date: September 2x08

1. Bingley plc

(a) Transactions with Collins plc

Under IAS 28, *Investments in Associates and Joint Ventures*, an associate is an entity over which the investor has significant influence and that is neither a subsidiary nor an interest in a joint venture. Significant influence is defined as the power to participate in the financial and operating policy decisions of the investee but is neither control nor joint control over those policies.

As Collins plc has a majority shareholder, Bingley plc does not exercise control over it. However, such ownership by another investor does not preclude an investor from having significant influence (IAS 28.5).

An investor who holds less than 20%, as is the case with Bingley plc's holding in Collins plc, is presumed not to have significant influence, unless such influence can be clearly demonstrated (IAS 28.5).

Bingley plc is, however, represented on the Board of Directors of Collins plc and thereby participates in all major operating and financial policy decisions of the company. Material transactions also regularly take place between the two companies. Accordingly, Bingley plc does exercise significant influence over Collins plc, and the latter company should be accounted for as an associate under IAS 28.

The investment in Collins plc should therefore be accounted for under the equity method in the consolidated financial statements of the Darcy plc group.

Under this method, the investment in an associate is initially recognised at cost in the financial statements of the Group, and the carrying amount is increased or decreased to recognise the investor's share of the profit or loss of the associate after the date of acquisition. The investor's share of the profit or loss of the associate is recognised in the investor's consolidated statement of comprehensive income. Distributions received reduce the carrying amount of the investment. Adjustments to the carrying amount may also be necessary for changes in the investor's proportionate interest in the investee, arising from changes in the investee's other comprehensive income. Such changes include those arising from the revaluation of property, and from foreign exchange translation differences. The investor's share of those changes is recognised in other comprehensive income of the investor (IAS 28.11).

Profits and losses resulting from transactions between an investor and an associate are recognised in the investor's financial statements only to the extent of unrelated investors' interests in the associate (IAS 28.22).

Accordingly, in relation to the development land sold by Bingley plc to Collins plc, 18% of the €200,000 profit made on the sale, i.e. €36,000, should be eliminated in the consolidated financial statements of the group.

This is a consolidation adjustment, and the following journal entry is required:

	DR €	CR €
Cost of sales – SOCI P/L	36,000	
Investment in associate		36,000

It is also worthwhile to consider how the sale of the development site will have been recorded by Bingley (and therefore also in the accounts of the Group). As Bingley is engaged in property developing, the sale of a land site will be included in revenue. It will also result in a reduction in inventory.

	DR €'000	CR €'000
Bank/receivables	2,000	
Revenue – SOCI P/L		2,000
Cost of sales	1,800	
Inventory		1,800

Disclosure of the transaction between Bingley plc and Collins plc is also required under IAS 24, Related Party Transactions, as follows:

- The nature of the relationship between the parties, i.e. investor and associate;
- The amount of the transactions, i.e. €2,000,000;
- Details in relation to outstanding balances at the year end; and
- Any provisions for doubtful debts and bad debts written off.

(b) *Transactions with Phillips plc*

The interest acquired by Bingley plc in Phillips plc during the period should be accounted for in accordance with IFRS 11 *Joint Arrangements*.

Under IFRS 11, a joint arrangement is defined as an arrangement in which two or more parties have joint control. This is clearly the case in relation to Phillips plc.

As Bingley and the other investor share joint control over the net assets of Phillips, the latter company is a joint venture.

As required by IFRS 11 *Joint Arrangements*, Bingley must account for its interest in Phillips using the equity method.

Under the **equity method**, the investment in Phillips plc would initially be recognised at cost, and the carrying amount increased or decreased to recognise the group's share of the post-acquisition change in the net assets of Phillips plc. The group statement of comprehensive income will recognise a share of the profit or loss of Phillips plc (IAS 28.10).

2.   Bennett plc

(a)   *Acquisition of industrial saw*

IAS 17, *Leases,* deals with the accounting treatment of operating and finance leases.

A finance lease is a lease that transfers substantially all of the risks and rewards incidental to ownership of an asset (IAS 17.4). The saw has an estimated life of four years, and the lease period is initially for the same period, while Bennett has an option to extend the lease by a further two years. Therefore, as the agreement transfers all of the risks and rewards of ownership of the saw to Bennett, this represents a finance lease.

Accounting treatment

At the *commencement of the lease term*, lessees shall recognise finance leases as assets and liabilities in their statement of financial position, at amounts equal to the fair value of the leased asset or, if lower, the present value of the minimum lease payments, each determined at the inception of the lease (IAS 17.20).

As the fair value of the industrial saw is not available, the present value of the minimum lease payments is used in this case.

IAS 17 requires that the minimum lease payments shall be apportioned between the finance charge and the reduction of the outstanding liability. The finance charge shall be allocated to each period so as to produce a constant periodic rate of interest on the remaining balance of the liability (IAS 17.25).

Workings

(i) *Present value of minimum lease payments*
Based on a discount rate of 12%:

		€
Year 0	5,000 × 1 =	5,000
Year 1	5,000 × .893 =	4,465
Year 2	5,000 × .797 =	3,985
Year 3	5,000 × .712 =	3,560
		17,010

(ii) *Initial record of the lease*

	DR	CR
	€	€
PPE	17,010	
Lease obligation – SOFP		17,010

(iii) *Allocation of lease payments between capital and interest*

Year End	Opening Capital Balance	Rental	Capital Repaid	Accrued Finance Charge @ 12%	Closing Capital Balance
31.12.07	17,010	(5,000)	5,000	1,441 (a)	12,010
31.12.08	12,010	(5,000)	3,559 (d)	1,014 (b)	8,451
31.12.09	8,451	(5,000)	3,986 (e)	535 (c)	4,465
31.12.10	4,465	(5,000)	4,465 (f)	0	

(a) $(17,010 - 5,000) \times 12\% = 1,441$

(b) $(13,451^* - 5,000) \times 12\% = 1,014$

(c) $(9,465 - 5,000) \times 12\% = 535$

(d) (5,000 – 1,441)   = 3,559
(e) (5,000 – 1,014)   = 3,986
(f) (5,000 – 535)   = 4,465

* 12,010 + 1,441 = 13,451

Extract from Statement of Comprehensive Income for the year ended 31 December 2x07

	€
Depreciation (17,010/4 Years)	4,253
Finance Charge	1,441

Extract from Statement of Financial Position as at 31 December 2x07

Non-current assets
Cost	17,010
Accumulated depreciation	(4,253)
Net book value	12,757

Non-current liabilities
Finance lease	8,451 (i.e. 5k + 5k) – (1,014 + 535)

Current liabilities
Finance lease	3,559
Accruals (Finance charge)	1,441

(b) Shipment of timber products

In relation to the shipment to the new customer, the products have been delivered to the customer with a limited right of return. Although the customer has not contacted the company to confirm its acceptance of the goods, the time period for return has elapsed before the year-end of the company. Accordingly, it must be assumed that the customer has accepted the goods and there is therefore no further uncertainty about the possibility of return (e.g. 2 (b) of Appendix to IAS 18).

It is therefore appropriate to recognise the revenue in the financial statements of Bennett plc for the year ended 31 December 2x07. The following journal is required:

	DR €'000	CR €'000
Trade receivables	220	
Revenue – SOCI P/L		220
(Being sales of goods to customer)		

In determining the accounting treatment, one should also consider whether any further information (e.g. the late return of the goods) is available after 31 December 2x07.

(c) Inventories

(i) Change in basis of inventory valuation

Under IAS 2, *Inventories,* inventories shall be measured at the lower of cost and net realisable value (IAS 2.9).

The cost of inventories of items that are ordinarily interchangeable should be assigned using the first-in, first-out or weighted average cost formula (IAS 2.25).

Bennett plc's large inventories of small 'Category C' products, that cannot be separately identified, fall within this category, and therefore one of the above cost formulas should be used. The use of the last-in, first-out (LIFO) formula is not permitted under IAS 2.

The inventories of the company at 31 December 2x07 should therefore be reduced by €110,000 to reflect the first-in, first-out basis of valuation. The following journal is required:

	DR €'000	CR €'000
Cost of sales – SOCI P/L	110	
Inventories – SOFP		110
(Being reduction in inventories to reflect the FIFO cost formula)		

A change from the LIFO basis of inventory valuation to the FIFO basis is the correction of an error, which must be treated in accordance with IAS 8, *Accounting Policies, Changes in Accounting Estimates and Errors.*

However, as the cost of these items did not move significantly in the past, it is likely that the FIFO and LIFO figures would not have been materially different. Therefore, it is not necessary to make a prior period adjustment.

(ii) Reversal of NRV write-down

Where the cost of inventories may not be recoverable, it is appropriate to write the inventories down below cost to net realisable value (IAS 2.28).

Bennett plc undertook such a write-down in the year ended 31 December 2x06 in relation to Product X items included in its inventories. However, market conditions have now changed and the items could be sold for more than cost at 31 December 2x07.

In these circumstances it is appropriate to reverse the write-down so that the new carrying amount is the lower of cost and the revised net realisable value. The reversal is limited to the amount of the original write-down to ensure that the inventories are not valued at an amount that is higher than their cost (IAS 2.33).

Such a reversal should be treated as a reduction in the amount of inventories recognised as an expense in the period in which the reversal occurs (IAS 2.34).

In this case, the original cost of the inventory of €190,000 should be reinstated.

The following journal is required:

	DR €'000	CR €'000
Inventories – SOFP	60	
Cost of sales – SOCI P/L		60

(Being reversal of NRV write-down due to changed circumstances)

(d)   Grant Assistance

Under IAS 20, *Accounting for Government Grants and Disclosure of Government Assistance,* government grants should not be recognised until there is reasonable assurance that:

- The entity will comply with the conditions attaching to them; and
- The grants will be received (IAS 20.7).

Government grants related to assets may be presented in the statement of financial position either by setting up the grant as deferred income or by deducting the grant in arriving at the carrying amount of the asset. The treatment of the grant as deferred income by Bennett plc is therefore appropriate (IAS 20.24).

Bennett plc has received a grant of €900,000 (€1,500,000 × 60%) during the year ended 31 December 2x07. The two conditions relevant to the grant are the hire of additional staff and the purchase of specified items of plant. Whilst the former condition has been met, the latter has been met in relation to only €720,000 (€1,200,000 x 60%) of the grant. As the purchase of further plant is subject to cashflow considerations, Bennett plc's compliance with the conditions is not yet assured.

Accordingly, €720,000 of the grant should be accounted for as a separate category of deferred income in the year ended 31 December 2x07. The remaining €180,000 of the grant should be accounted for in the year to 31 December 2x08 when the directors incur the matching capital expenditure.

Under IAS 20, government grants should be recognised as income over the periods necessary to match them with the related costs which they are intended to compensate, on a systematic basis (IAS 20.12).

Grants related to depreciable assets, as is the case here, are recognised as income over the periods and in the proportion in which the depreciation on those assets is charged (IAS 20.17).

As the plant is depreciated on a straight-line basis at 8% per annum, and a full year's depreciation has been deducted in the year to 31 December 2x07, a matching 8% of the grant of €720,000, i.e. €57,600, should be released from deferred income and recognised as income in the financial statements for the year.

The following journals are required to reflect the above treatment:

	DR €'000	CR €'000
Deferred income – SOFP	180	
Other creditors		180
(Being removal of government grant for which conditions not yet satisfied)		
Deferred income – SOFP	57.6	
Amortisation of government grants – SOCI P/L		57.6
(Being release of government grant to match with depreciation charge)		

The disclosures required are as follows:

- The accounting policy adopted for government grants, including the methods of presentation in the financial statements;
- The nature and extent of government grants recognised in the financial statements, and an indication of other forms of government assistance from which the entity has directly benefited; *and*
- Unfulfilled conditions and other contingencies attaching to government assistance that has been recognised (IAS 20.39).

Drafting of disclosures

Accounting Policy note:

Government grants receivable on additions to tangible non-current assets are credited to the Government Grants Account and are allocated to the Statement of Comprehensive Income over the estimated effective lives of the assets concerned, in line with the depreciation policy of the company.

	€
Balance at beginning of year	x
Receivable for year	720,000
Released to statement of comprehensive income	(57,600)
Balance at end of year	x

The company received government grants of €900,000 during the year to aid the purchase of certain items of fixed plant required in relation to the planned expansion of the manufacturing business. At the year-end, the conditions in relation to €720,000 of this grant had been fulfilled and accordingly this amount has been recognised in the financial statements. The remaining €180,000 will be recognised when further plant is purchased.

SOLUTION TO ROCKET GROUP

Memorandum

From: **A. Senior**

To: **Group Financial Director, Rocket plc**

Date: **1 March 2x08**

Further to our recent meeting, I have detailed below my views in respect of accounting issues arising in respect of the financial statements for the year ended 31 December 2x07.

(a) *Launch Plc*

    (i) *Work in progress inventory*

Work in progress inventory should be valued at the lower of cost and net realisable value (IAS 2.9). Cost is defined as the cost of purchase, costs of conversion and other costs incurred in bringing the inventories to their present location and condition (IAS 2.10). Costs of conversion include costs directly related to the units of production such as direct labour. They also include a systematic allocation of fixed and variable production overheads (IAS 2.12).

The cost of the carpet inventory at 31 December 2x07 is therefore computed as follows:

	€'000
Materials (200 units @ €1,500 x 75%)	225
Labour (200 units @ €600 x 75%)	90
Fixed production overheads (note 1)	47
Total cost	362

Note 1: The allocation of fixed production overheads to the costs of conversion is usually based on the normal capacity of the production facilities (IAS 2.13). However, in periods of abnormally high production, the amount of fixed overhead allocated to each unit of production is decreased so that inventories are not measured above cost (IAS 2.13).

During 2x07, LAUNCH produced 12,000 finished carpets, compared to a normal output level of 10,000. On the basis that 12,000 represents an abnormally high production figure, fixed production overheads should be allocated to production in a way that avoids inventories being measured in excess of their cost. This can be achieved by allocating overheads based on the actual level of production achieved.

The fixed production overhead content of the carpets that were partially completed at 31 December 2x07, should be computed as follows:

Total fixed production overheads	€3.8 million

Production overhead per fully completed carpet, based on actual output of 12,000 carpets (€3.8 million/12,000)	€317

Therefore, the amount of fixed production overheads to be included in the cost of the 200 carpets, which are on average 75% complete, is computed as follows:

$$200 \times .75 \times €317 = €47,550$$

IAS 23 *Borrowing Costs* requires that costs that are directly attributable to the acquisition, construction or production of a qualifying asset, shall be capitalised as part of the cost of that asset (IAS 23.8). A qualifying asset is an asset that necessarily takes a substantial period of time to get ready for its intended use or sale (IAS 23.5). As 10,000 carpets are produced annually by Launch, this category of asset does not represent a qualifying asset. Thus, the interest costs should be expensed as they are incurred.

Distribution costs, sales commissions and administration costs are not costs related to the production of the carpets, and therefore they are not included in the valuation of inventory.

Carpet manufactured for the Regency Hotel

One of the carpets, which was 75% complete at the 31 December 2x07, was produced for the Regency Hotel, which closed in early January 2x08. The carpet can however be sold to another customer, giving rise to the following **net realisable value:**

	€
Selling price	3,000
Less:	
Completion costs (€362,000/200 × 1/3)	(603)
Selling and distribution costs	(800)
Net realisable value	1,597
Cost of carpet (€362,000/200)	1,810

Cost 1 carpet

Therefore, the Regency Hotel carpet should be valued at its net realisable value of €1,597.

Journal entries

	DR	CR
	€	€
Closing inventory – SOFP	362,000	
Cost of sales		362,000
(Being work in progress inventory at 31 December 2x07)		
Cost of sales	213	
Closing inventory – SOFP		213
(Being restatement of carpet to net realisable value i.e. €1,810 – €1,597)		

(ii) *Carpet ends and floor mats*

The carpet ends and floor mats represent a minor by-product, whose cost is not separable from the company's main product. In accordance with IAS 2, the inventories of such by-products, when immaterial, may be measured at net realisable value, and this value is deducted from the cost of the main product (IAS 2.14).

In the case of Launch Plc, the following journal entries are required:

	DR €	CR €
Bank	130,000	
Revenue		130,000
(Being sales of carpet ends and floor mats during 2x08)		
Inventory of carpet ends and floor mats – SOFP	25,000	
Cost of sales		25,000
(Being NRV of by-product offset against the production costs of Launch Plc's main product)		

(iii) *Inventory of wool*

The wool inventory held by Launch Plc at 31 December 2x07 has a cost of €600,000, and a NRV of only €200,000. However, it is anticipated that this wool will be used for the production of carpets which are expected to be sold above cost.

Materials held for use in the production of inventories are **not** written down below cost if the finished products in which they will be incorporated are expected to be sold at or above cost (IAS 2.32). Consequently, the wool inventory of Launch Plc should be included in the financial statements at cost on 31 December 2x07. As Launch Plc has already reduced the inventory to €450,000, this write down in value should be reversed as follows:

	DR €	CR €
Inventory of materials – SOFP	150,000	
Cost of sales		150,000
(Being reversal of write down of wool inventory)		

(iv) Sale and leaseback

(I) Factory lease

IAS 17 *Leases* defines a finance lease as a lease that transfers substantially all the risks and rewards incidental to ownership of an asset. In the case of the factory building it is clear that the lease agreement qualifies as a finance lease. This is so, as the lease term of 50 years is in line with the asset's estimated useful life, and Launch Plc has an option to extend the lease for a further 30 years by making a nominal annual payment.

Where a sale and leaseback transaction results in a finance lease, IAS 17 states that any excess of proceeds over the carrying amount of the asset is deferred and amortised over the lease term (IAS 17.59). Thus, the following journal entries will be required:

	DR €'000	CR €'000	
Bank	12,000		*Sale of*
Buildings		10,000	*Factory* ✓
Deferred income – SOFP		2,000	
(Being sale of factory on 1 January 2x07)			
Revaluation surplus – SOFP	4,000		*€ 6million – €4u*
Retained earnings – SOFP		4,000	✓
(Being transfer of capital surplus on factory to realised reserves, following the sale of the asset)			
Buildings	12,000		*Finance* ✓
Lease obligation – SOFP		12,000	*lease*
(Being finance lease signed on 1 January 2x07)			
Lease obligation P/L(OCI)	500		*Payment of*
Bank		500	*lease* ✓
(Being lease instalment paid on 1 January 2x07)			
Depreciation expense – SOCI P/L	240		*Dep* ✓
Accumulated depreciation		240	*12,000*
(Being depreciation of factory for 2x07)			*50*
Lease interest – SOCI P/L	260		
Lease obligation – SOFP		260	
(Being lease interest charge for 2x07)			

Deferred income – SOFP   40
Amortisation of deferred income – SOCI P/L   40
(Being amortisation of deferred income
over lease term, i.e. €2m/50)

Lecture note: It should be noted that the use of the straight line method would not normally be permitted by IAS 17 for the amortisation of interest in a finance lease.

(II)   Car park

The car park which is the subject of the sale and leaseback agreement is on a 3-acre site. This car park is in the nature of land, and the asset consequently has an indefinite life. It is appropriate therefore to treat the lease as an operating lease, which is defined by IAS 17 as a lease other than a finance lease (IAS 17.4).

Where a sale and leaseback transaction results in an operating lease, and it is clear that the transaction is carried out at fair value, the profit or loss should be recognised immediately (IAS 17.61). Thus, the following journal entries will be required:

	DR €'000	CR €'000
Bank	9,000	
Land		7,000
Profit on disposal – SOCI P/L		2,000
(Being disposal of car park on 1 January 2x07)		
Revaluation surplus – SOFP	3,000	
Retained earnings – SOFP		3,000
(Being transfer of capital surplus on car park to realised reserves, following the sale of the asset)		
Lease charge – SOCI P/L	400	
Bank		400
(Being lease instalment paid by Launch Plc on 1 January 2x07)		

(b)   Space Plc

The following journal entries are required in respect of the purchase and disposal of the building by Space Plc:

	DR €'000	CR €'000
Building	6,000	
Bank		6,000
(Being purchase of building on 1 January 2x03)		
Depreciation expense	120	
Accumulated depreciation		120
(Being depreciation of building for 2x03)		
Depreciation expense	120	
Accumulated depreciation		120
(Being depreciation of building for 2x04)		
Accumulated depreciation	240	
Building		240
(Being elimination of accumulated depreciation prior to impairment write down)		
Impairment write down – SOCI P/L	1,760	
Building		1,760
(Being impairment write down on 1 January 2x05)		
Depreciation expense	83	
Accumulated depreciation		83
(Being depreciation of building for 2x05, based on a net book value of €4 million/48 years)		
Depreciation expense	83	
Accumulated depreciation		83
(Being depreciation of building for 2x06, based on a net book value of €4 million/48 years)		
Accumulated depreciation	166	
Building		166
(Being elimination of accumulated depreciation prior to revaluation)		

Building	3,166	
Reversal of previous impairment – SOCI P/L		1,686*
Revaluation surplus – SOCI OCI		1,480

(Being revaluation of building to €7 million
on 1 Jan. 2x07)

* The write back to the income statement is restricted to the original write-down, less the additional depreciation that would have been charged, had the asset not become impaired in the first place (i.e. €1.76m less ((€120k − €83k) × 2)).

Bank	8,000	
Building		7,000
Profit on disposal – SOCI P/L		1,000*

(Being sale of building to Launch Plc on 31 Dec. 2x07)

Revaluation surplus – SOFP	1,480	
Retained earnings – SOFP		1,480

(Being transfer of revaluation surplus to retained earnings, on
sale of the building on 31 December 2x07)

* Subject to considerations of materiality, in accordance with IAS 1 *Presentation of Financial Statements*, the profit on disposal should be separately disclosed either on the face of the statement of comprehensive income or in the notes (IAS 1.97). This may be required in the financial statements of Space plc and the consolidated financial statements of the Group.

Space Plc and Launch Plc are members of the same group, and thus they are related parties, as defined by IAS 24 (IAS 24.9 (a) (i)). Thus, the sale of the building by Space to Launch constitutes a material related party transaction, and disclosure should be made in the separate financial statements of both Space Plc and Launch Plc. No disclosure is required in the group financial statements, as the transaction will be cancelled on consolidation.

Disclosure of the following details is required (IAS 24.17):

- Description of the relationship between the related parties (fellow subsidiaries of Rocket Plc)
- The amount of the transaction (sale of land for €8 million)
- Any other elements of the transaction necessary for an understanding of the financial statements
- The amounts due or from the related parties at the statement of financial position date.

SOLUTION TO
TELFER GROUP

Memorandum

From: **A. Senior**

To: **Group Financial Director, Telfer Industrial Group**

Date: **1 July 2x09**

Further to our recent meeting, I have detailed below my views in respect of accounting issues arising in respect of the financial statements of the Telfer group of companies.

(1) Acquisition of Summit Limited

The acquisition of Summit Limited is achieved by what is termed a 'step acquisition' by IFRS 3 *Business Combinations*. This has the following implications in this case:

(i) *Associate stage*
Telfer Holdings Limited had significant influence over Summit Limited as and from its purchase of a 25% shareholding in that company on the 31 May 2x07. Summit Limited is defined as an associate of Telfer Holdings Limited at that date (IAS 28.3). Summit Limited is therefore accounted for under the equity method in the consolidated financial statements of the Telfer Group, as and from that date (IAS 28.16).

The following journal entries are required in the financial statements of the Telfer Group:

	DR €'000	CR €'000
Investment in Summit Limited	2,500	
Bank		2,500
(Being purchase of 25% stake in Summit Limited)		
Investment in Summit Limited	250	
Retained earnings		250
(Being the Telfer Group share of the retained earnings of Summit for the year ended 31 May 2x08: ((€8m − €7m) × 25%))		

our share of profits of associte nt group ae entited to.

2,750

(ii)   Subsidiary stage

On the 31 May 2x08, Telfer Holdings Limited acquired a further 65% of the shares in Summit Limited. IFRS 3 requires that, where a business combination is achieved in stages, the acquirer must remeasure its previously held equity interest at acquisition date fair value (IFRS 3.42). The resulting gain or loss, if any, should be recognised in profit or loss (IFRS 3.42).

Previously held equity interest in Summit at acquisition date fair value	€2.30m
Amount at which Summit was included in the financial statements of the group (€2.5m + €.25m)	€2.75m
Loss on remeasurement	€0.45m

previously held @ 2.3

invest 7m sub above

cash → 2.75 conser

Thus, a loss of €.45m will be recorded in the financial statements of the Telfer Group for the year ended 31 May 2x08.

Acquisition-related costs should be accounted for by the acquirer as an expense in the year ended 31 May 2x08 (IFRS 3.53).

Calculation of Goodwill

The following journal entries are required in the financial statements of the Telfer Group:

	DR €'000	CR €'000
Loss on remeasurement – SOCI P/L	450	
Investment in Summit Limited		450
(Being remeasurement of previously held equity interest)		
Identifiable net assets	9,000	
Bank		7,800 *Cash conside*
Investment in Summit Limited		2,300 *previously held*
Non-controlling interest* (€9m × 10%)		~~1,000~~
Goodwill **	2,000	900
Acquisition-related expenses – SOCI P/L of the Telfer Group for year ended 31 May 2x08	200	
Bank/Creditors		200
(Being acquisition costs incurred by Telfer Holdings Limited)		

* Non-controlling interest is computed above as a share of the fair value of the identifiable net assets of Summit Limited at acquisition date. IFRS 3 also permits non-controlling interest to be computed at its fair value (IFRS 3 Appendix B.44).

** IFRS 3 requires that goodwill is measured as the excess of (a) over (b) (IFRS 3.32):

(a) the aggregate of:

proportate basis

    (i)   the consideration transferred (€7.8m)

    (ii) the amount of any non-controlling interest in the acquiree (€.9m) *netAssets × NCI (10%) = 9000 × 10% = .9m*

FVamt (Given)

    (iii) in a business combination achieved in stages, the acquisition date fair value of the acquirer's previously held equity interest in the acquiree (€2.3m) *→ not getting 90% in one go → previously hold 25%*

• if do @ FV must then remove % NCI amt

(b) the net of the acquisition-date amounts of the identifiable assets acquired and the liabilities assumed (measured in accordance with IFRS 3) (€9m)

Thus, goodwill = (€7.8m + €.9m + €2.3m) − €9m
                = €2m

(iii) Disclosure

Appendix B of IFRS 3 requires that an acquirer shall disclose specific information for each business combination that occurs during the reporting period (IFRS 3 Appendix B.64).

The following disclosure note, relating to the acquisition of Summit Limited, is based on the illustrative examples in IFRS 3:

Para. ref.		€'000
B64 (a-d)	On 31 May 2x07 Telfer Holdings acquired 25% of the outstanding ordinary shares of Summit Limited. On 31 May 2x08 Telfer Holdings acquired 65% of Summit Limited and obtained control of that company. As a result of the acquisition, the Telfer Group will have an increased presence in the high margin industrial components market, which is an important and expanding market.	
B64 (e)	The goodwill of €2 million, arising from the acquisition, consists largely of the increased market opportunities from combining the operations of Summit Limited and the Telfer Group.	

if

Para. ref.		€'000
B64 (k)	The following table summarises the consideration paid for Summit Limited and the amounts of the assets acquired and liabilities assumed at the acquisition date, as well as the fair value at the acquisition date of the non-controlling interest in Summit Limited:	
	At 31 May 2x08	
	Consideration	
B64 (f)(i)	Cash	7,800
B64 p (i)	Fair value of Telfer's equity interest in Summit before the business combination	2,300
		10,100
B64 (m)	Acquisition-related costs (included in the Telfer Group's statement of comprehensive income for the year ended 31 May 2x08)	200
B64 (i)	Recognised amounts of identifiable assets acquired and liabilities assumed	9,000
B64 (o)	Non-controlling interest in Summit Limited	(900)
	Goodwill	2,000
		10,100

(iv) Disposal of shares

At the 31 May 2x08, Telfer Holdings Limited held 90% of the shares in Summit Limited. On the 28 February 2x09, a 20% stake in Summit Limited was sold, realising cash proceeds of €3 million.

IFRS 10 requires that, when changes in a parent's ownership interest in a subsidiary do not result in a loss of control, these changes are accounted for within shareholders' equity as transactions with owners acting in their capacity as owners (IFRS 10.23).

No gain or loss is recognised on such transactions, and goodwill is not re-measured. Any difference between the change in non-controlling interest and the fair value of consideration received is recognised directly in equity and attributed to the owners of the parent (IFRS 10, Appendix B, para. 96).

The following journal entries will be required in the financial statements of the Telfer Group:

	DR €'000	CR €'000
Bank	3,000	
Non-controlling interest*		2,015
Equity reserves – SOFP**		985

* (20% x fair value of net assets of Summit at 31 May 2x08) +
(20% x profits of Summit for 9 months of the year ended 31 May 2x09)

$$= (20\% \times €9 \text{ million}) + (20\% \times €1,430,000 \times 9/12)$$

$$= €2,015,000$$

** The gain on disposal of €985,000 will be shown in the SOCIE for the year ended 31 May 2x09 as an amount attributable to owners of the parent.

(2) Property Asset

IFRS 5; Asset held for sale.

(i) Purchase of building

The building purchased by Rampton Limited for €2 million on the 1 June 2x06 would have been classified as a non-current asset at that time. On the 31 May 2x07, the property was restated at €2.5 million under the revaluation model of IAS 16.

The following journal entries would have been required in the financial statements of Rampton Limited in the year ended 31 May 2x07:

	DR €'000	CR €'000
Buildings	2,000	
Bank		2,000
(Being purchase of building on the 1 June 2x06)		

Depreciation expense   *Debit Exp*   40
Accumulated depreciation   40
(Being depreciation of building for y/e 31 May 2x07)

Accumulated depreciation   40
Building   40
(Being elimination of accumulated depreciation at
  time of revaluation)

Disposal

| 50 |
| 500 |

540

Building   540
Revaluation surplus – SOCI OCI   540
(Being revaluation of building at 31 May 2x07)

(ii) Non-current asset held for sale

At the 31 May 2x08 it was decided to dispose of the building. IFRS 5 states *To bring As Back to IAS* that an entity shall classify a non-current asset as being held for sale if its carrying amount will be recovered principally through a sale transaction rather *recoveable* than through continuing use (IFRS 5.6). On the assumption that the build- *amt v* ing satisfies the further criteria of IFRS 5.7–5.8, it should be reclassified as *Carrying* an asset held for sale at the 31 May 2x08. *amt*

Prior to reclassification as held for sale, IFRS 5 requires that the building be *→if you* accounted for in accordance with applicable IFRSs (IFRS 5.18). Thus, in *had no* accordance with IAS 16, depreciation should be fully up to date, and the *moved in* building should be restated at its fair value of €3 million. *the first*

The following journal entries would have been required in the financial *place* statements of Rampton Limited in the year ended 31 May 2x08:

	DR €'000	CR €'000
Depreciation expense	51	
Accumulated depreciation		51
(Being depreciation of building for y/e 31 May 2x08 i.e. €2.5 million/49)		

50 years – 1 year already dep for.

Accumulated depreciation	51	
Building		51
(Being elimination of accumulated depreciation at time of revaluation)		

Building	551	
Revaluation surplus – SOCI OCI		551

(Being revaluation of building at 31 May 2x08)

Asset held for sale	3,000	
Building – non-current asset		3,000

(Being classification of the building as an asset held for sale)

Revaluation surplus – SOCI OCI	100	
Asset held for sale		100

(Being set off of selling costs, after the asset is classified
as held for sale, so that the asset is valued at fair
value less costs to sell, in accordance with IFRS 5)

The Standard does not state whether this amount should be charged to profit or loss, or to OCI.

(iii) Change to a plan of sale

At the 31 May 2x09 the property was withdrawn from sale.

IFRS 5 requires that, if the criteria to be classified as held for sale are no longer met, an entity shall cease to classify an asset as held for sale (IFRS 5.26).

Such an asset (or disposal group) should be measured at the *lower of:*

(I) its carrying amount before it was classified as held for sale, adjusted for any depreciation, amortisation or revaluations that would have been recognised had the asset (or disposal group) not been classified as held for sale, **and**

(II) its recoverable amount (i.e. higher of fair value less costs to sell, and value in use) at the date of the decision not to sell (IFRS 5.27).

The asset that is being held for sale by Rampton Limited should therefore be measured at the **lower of:**

(I) €3 million less one year's depreciation (€3 million/48) = €2,937,500, and

(II) the asset's recoverable amount (i.e. higher of fair value less costs to sell of €1.8 million and value in use of €1.5 million).

The asset should therefore be valued at its recoverable amount of €1.8 million.

Any required adjustment to the carrying value of a non-current asset that ceases to be classified as held for sale should be included in profit or loss for continuing operations (IFRS 5.28). However, the adjustment should be treated as a revaluation increase or decrease if the asset had been revalued in accordance with IAS 16 before classification as held for sale (IFRS 5.28).

The following journal entry is therefore required in the financial statements of Rampton Limited for the year ended 31 May 2x09:

	DR €'000	CR €'000
Building	2,900	
Asset held for sale		2,900
(Being re-classification of building when it ceases to be held for sale)		
Revaluation surplus – SOCI OCI (540k + 551k – 100k)	991	
Impairment loss – SOCI P/L	109	
Building (2.9m – 1.8m)		1,100
(Being adjustment on asset that ceases to be classified as held for sale)		

(3) Intra-Group Sales

IFRS 10 requires that profits and losses resulting from intragroup transactions that are recognised in assets, such as inventory, should be eliminated in full (IFRS 10, Appendix B, para. 86).

Rampton Limited and Brink Limited are both subsidiaries of Telfer Holdings. Thus, to the extent that goods purchased from Brink Limited are held in inventory by Rampton at the 31 May 2x09, any intragroup profit or loss must be eliminated.

To reduce sales: DEBIT

It must be considered however that Brink Limited will have incurred a corporation tax charge on profits earned on goods sold to Rampton. Thus, from a group perspective, although the intragroup profit on goods held in inventory must be eliminated, the tax charge remains.

Therefore, a group tax charge is being recorded in advance of the recognition of the related profit. This represents a deductible temporary difference, as defined by IAS 12 *Income Taxes*.

The following journal entries are required in the group financial statements at the 31 May 2x09:

	DR €'000	CR €'000
Revenue	12,000	
Cost of sales		12,000
(Being elimination of intragroup sales)		
Cost of sales	800	
Inventory – SOFP		800
(Being elimination of unrealised intragroup profit on inventory: 12m x 1/3 x 20%)		
Deferred tax asset – SOFP	160	
Deferred tax credit – SOCI P/L		160
(Being deferred tax credit on unrealised intragroup profit on inventory i.e. 800k x 20%)		

[handwritten annotations: "Deferred Tax asset 'less tax in future (+)"; "roman shoe"; "profit will never be realised, so will never have to pay future tax: less Tax: Asset"]

Disclosure

As Rampton Limited and Brink Limited are members of the same group, they are defined as related parties by IAS 24 (IAS 24.9). Sales by Brink to Rampton therefore are related party transactions. Subject to the amounts involved being material, the following disclosure notes will be required:

Group financial statements

As intragroup sales are cancelled in the consolidated financial statements, no disclosure is required.

Financial statements of Rampton Limited

Brink Limited is a related party of Rampton Limited, by virtue of both parties being members of the Telfer Group. Sales by Brink to Rampton amounted to €12 million during the year ended 31 May 2x09. The amount outstanding at 31 May 2x09 in the statement of financial position of Rampton in respect of these transactions was €xxx.

(4) Sale of goods

IAS 18 Revenue requires that revenue should be measured at the fair value of the consideration received or receivable (IAS 18.9). IAS 18 also states that when the inflow of cash is deferred, the fair value of the consideration may be less than the nominal amount of cash receivable (IAS 18.11).

When the arrangement effectively constitutes a financing transaction, the fair value of the consideration is determined by discounting all future receipts using an imputed rate of interest (IAS 18.11).

The difference between the fair value and the nominal amount of the consideration is recognised as interest revenue (IAS 18.11).

In the case of Rampton Limited, it is clear that nine units of product have been sold on normal credit terms of two months. Sales of these items should be recorded without adjustment to fair value. In respect of the other item however, a year's interest-free credit has been allowed. As this transaction effectively constitutes a financing transaction, the consideration should be discounted to fair value at a rate of 10%.

The following journal entries will be required in the financial statements of Rampton Limited during May 2x09:

	DR €'000	CR €'000
Trade receivables	900	
Revenue		900
(Being the sale of 9 integrated waste management systems)		
Trade receivables	90.9	
Revenue		90.9
(Being the sale of 1 system on extended credit: €100k/1.1)		
Cost of sales	800	
Inventory – SOFP		800
(Being the cost of 10 waste management systems)		

$100 \times .2$
$= 20,000$

$= 100 - 20$
$= 80 \times 10$
$= 800$

The following journal entry will be required in the financial statements of Rampton Limited during the year ended 31 May 2x10:

	DR €'000	CR €'000
Bank	100	
Trade receivables		90.9
Interest revenue – SOCI P/L		9.1

(Being cash received in respect of sale on extended credit)

SOLUTION TO CAMPBELL GROUP

Memorandum

From: **Sarah Mulhern**

To: **Martin Mangan, Group Chief Accountant**

Date: **1 February 2x11**

Further to our recent meeting, I have detailed below my views in respect of accounting issues arising in respect of the financial statements of the Campbell Group of companies.

The following issues are addressed:

(1) Computation of the basic and diluted EPS

(2) Employee benefits

(3) Additional disclosures for publicly listed companies

(4) Workings are contained in Appendix 1

(1) Computation of Basic and Diluted EPS

Basic earnings per share shall be calculated by dividing profit attributable to ordinary equity holders of the parent entity (the numerator) by the weighted average number of ordinary shares outstanding (the denominator) during the period (IAS 33.10).

Applying this requirement of IAS 33, the basic and diluted EPS are computed as follows:

(a) Year ended 31 December 2x10

	Earnings	No. of Shares	EPS	Incremental EPS
	€'m	M		
Basic EPS				
(W1) & (W2)	1,180	2,247	**52.51c** *Basic EPS*	
Potential ordinary shares (W4):				
- Options	Nil	30		Nil *(Dilutive)*
	1,180	2,277	51.82c	
- 8% Conv. Debentures	28	250		11.2c. *(Dilutive)*
Diluted EPS	1,208	2,527.2	**47.8c** *Diluted EPS*	

(b) Year ended 31 December 2x09 – Restated EPS

Basic EPS for 2009 as originally reported = €850m/800m shares (W1) = 106.25c

2009 EPS	x	Bonus Factor	x	Rights Multiplier (W3)	EPS Restated for 2009
106.25c	x	1/2	x	2.40/2.50	51.0c

Previously reported EPS for 2x09, restated for bonus issue and the bonus element of the rights issue that took place during 2x10

(2) Employee Benefits

(a) Short-term employee benefits

IAS 19 defines short-term employee benefits as "... employee benefits (other than termination benefits) that are due to be settled within 12 months after the end of the period in which the employees render the related service" (IAS 19.7).

Short-term benefits should be recognised as:
- a liability, after deducting any amount already paid (IAS 19.10 (a))
- an expense, unless another Standard requires or permits the inclusion of the benefits in the cost of an asset (IAS 19.10 (b)).

The Campbell Group has incurred a total of €16.5m during December 2x10 in the provision of short-term employee benefits. In accordance with IAS 19, €15.3m should be recorded in profit or loss and either credited to bank or accrued as a liability at 31 December 2x10.

IAS 16 Property, Plant and Equipment requires that directly attributable costs be included in the cost of an asset (IAS 16.16). IAS 16 specifies the costs of employee benefits arising from the construction of property as being an example of attributable costs for this purpose (IAS 16.17). Thus, the costs incurred by the Campbell Group in respect of the factory extension should be capitalised as part of the cost of land and buildings.

The following journal entry is required:

	€'m	€'m
Wages & salaries – SOCI P/L	15.3	
Land and buildings	1.2	
Bank		10.4
Trade and other payables (€3.6m + €1.1m + €0.6m + €0.8m)		6.1

IAS 19 also requires that an entity should recognise the cost of **bonus payments** when:
- the entity has a present legal or constructive obligation to make such payments as a result of past events; and
- a reliable estimate of the obligation can be made (IAS 19.19).

In respect of the commitments to staff in Auto Limited, bonus payments of €1.8m should be recognised as follows:

	€'m	€'m
Wages & salaries – SOCI P/L	1.8	
Trade and other payables – SOFP		1.8

(b) Post-employment benefits

(i) Defined contribution plan

IAS 19 requires that, when an employee has rendered service to an entity during a period, the entity should recognise the contribution payable to a defined contribution plan in exchange for that service (IAS 19.51):
- as a liability, after deducting any contribution already paid; and
- as an expense.

Thus, the following journal entry is required in respect of the defined contribution plan of the Campbell Group:

	€'m	€'m
Wages & salaries – SOCI P/L	120	
Bank		95
Trade and other payables – SOFP		25

Employee contributions will normally be a deduction from gross salary costs, and neither an expense nor a liability will arise from the perspective of the Campbell Group.

(ii) Defined benefit plan

Recognition of actuarial gains and losses in the period in which they occur

IAS 19 *Employee Benefits* requires that actuarial gains and losses are recognised in other comprehensive income in the period in which they occur. So as to prepare the financial statements of the Group for the year ended 31 December 2x10, it will be necessary to compute the following amounts in respect of the defined benefit pension plan:

- Charge to profit or loss for the year ended 31 December 2x10
- Pension liability at 31 December 2x10
- Actuarial gains/losses for the year ended 31 December 2x10.

- **Charge to profit or loss for the year ended 31 December 2x10**

  The defined benefit expense for the period can be computed as follows:

	€'m
Net interest	20 ✓
Present value of current service cost for the year	390 ✓
Defined benefit expense for the period	410

- **Pension liability at 31 December 2x10**

Present value of defined benefit obligation at year end	2,300 ✓
Fair value of assets of plan at year end	1,650 ✓
Defined benefit liability at 31 December 2x10	650

  The defined benefit liability has increased by €50m during the year (i.e. from €600m to €650m). ✓

- **Actuarial gains/losses for year ended 31 December 2x10**

  Actuarial gain/loss on <u>obligations</u> of pension plan:

	€'m
Present value of defined benefit obligation at 1 January 2x10	1,680 ✓
Present value of current service cost for the year	390 ✓
Interest cost	230 ✓
Benefits paid during the year	(150) ✓
	2,150
Actuarial loss (balancing figure)	150
Present value of defined benefit obligation at end of year	2,300 ✓

  The above actuarial loss of €150m will be included in other comprehensive income for the year ended 31 December 2x10.

Actuarial gain/loss on <u>assets</u> of pension plan:

	€'m	
Fair value of assets of plan at 1 January 2x10	1,080	✓
Employer contributions	400	✓
Expected return on assets of plan	210	
Benefits paid during year	(150)	
	1,540	
Actuarial gain (balancing figure)	110	
Fair value of assets of plan at end of year	1,650	

The actuarial gain of €110m on the assets of the plan will be recognised as part of other comprehensive income for the year ended 31 December 2x10.

Consequently, there will be a net charge of €40m in other comprehensive income for the year ended 31 December 2x10 (i.e. actuarial loss of €150m, less an actuarial gain of €110m).

- **Journal entries**

  The following journal entries will be required for the year ended 31 December 2x10:

	DR €'m	CR €'m
Defined benefit assets	400	
Bank		400
(Being employer contributions for the year)		
Defined benefit obligation — SOFP	150	
Defined benefit assets		150
(Being benefits paid for the year)		
Defined benefit assets	210	
Net interest – SOCI P/L		210
(Being expected return on assets)		
Net interest – SOCI P/L	230	
Defined benefit obligation – SOFP		230

(Being interest cost for year)

Current service costs – SOCI P/L	390	
Defined benefit obligation – SOFP		390

(Being current service cost for year)

Actuarial loss – SOCI OCI	150	
Defined benefit obligation		150

(Being actuarial loss for year on defined
benefit pension plan)

Defined benefit assets	110	
Actuarial gain – SOCI OCI		110

(Being actuarial gain on assets of plan)

The journal entries above will lead to a net increase of €50m* in the defined benefit pension liability at 31 December 2x10. This will increase the pension liability in the statement of financial position from €600m to €650m.

* Increase in obligation (€390m – €150m + €230m + €150m) less increase in assets (€210m + €400m – €150m + €110m)

(3) Additional disclosures arising for a listed company

(a) Operating Segments

IFRS 8 *Operating Segments* applies to entities whose equity instruments are traded on a stock exchange (IFRS 8.2). Thus, the Campbell Group, whose shares are listed on the Dublin and London exchanges, comes within the scope of the Standard.

An operating segment is defined as a component of an entity (IFRS 8.5):
- that engages in business activities from which it may earn revenues and incur expenses
- whose operating results are regularly reviewed to make decisions when allocating resources and assessing performance, and
- for which discrete financial information is available.

The strategy of the Campbell Group has been to form a separate company for each main area of operation, with separate subsidiaries being responsible for car sales, car hire, valeting and repairs, leasing and hire purchase, and sales of motor accessories. It seems reasonable to conclude that each of these subsidiaries represents an operating segment of the Campbell Group.

IFRS 8 requires an entity to report separately information about an operating segment that meets any of the following quantitative thresholds (IFRS 8.13):

(i)   Its reported revenue is 10% or more of the combined revenue of all operating segments.

(ii) The amount of its reported profit or loss is 10% or more of the greater of (I) the combined profit of all operating segments that did not report a loss and (II) the combined reported loss of all operating segments that reported a loss.

(iii) Its assets are 10% or more of the combined assets of all operating segments.

Disclosure

The Campbell Group is required to disclose the factors used to identify its reportable segments and the types of products and services from which each reportable segment derives its revenue (IFRS 8.22). The Group will also be required to disclose the profit or loss and total assets for each of its reportable segments (IFRS 8.23).

The following additional disclosures are required for each reportable segment if the information is regularly reported to the chief operating decision-maker (IFRS 8.23):

(i)   segment liabilities

(ii) the following items of income and expense:

- revenues from external customers and from other operating segments of the Group
- interest revenue and interest expense
- depreciation, amortisation and other material non-cash items
- items of income and expense that are sufficiently material to warrant separate disclosure

- the Group's interest in the profit or loss of associates and joint ventures accounted for by the equity method
- income tax expense or income.

IFRS 8 also requires entities to provide a number of reconciliations and to make certain entity-wide disclosures. The latter disclosures are not required if the information has already been provided as part of the information on reportable segments.

(b)   Interim financial reporting   IAS 34

As the Campbell Group is listed on the Dublin and London stock markets, under Stock Exchange rules it is required to present interim financial statements. IAS 34 *Interim Financial Reporting* also encourages publicly traded entities to:
- provide interim financial reports at least as of the end of the first half of their financial year; and
- make their interim financial reports available not later than 60 days after the end of the interim period (IAS 34.1).

The Campbell Group has the option of publishing a complete set of financial statements in its interim financial report (IAS 34.7). Alternatively, it may provide a condensed set of financial statements consisting, at a minimum, of the following components (IAS 34.8):
- a condensed statement of financial position
- a condensed statement of comprehensive income
- a condensed statement of changes in equity
- a condensed statement of cash flows; and
- selected explanatory notes.

As the ordinary shares of the Campbell Group are quoted on the stock market, basic and diluted earnings per share for the interim period should be presented in the statement of comprehensive income, whether condensed or otherwise (IAS 34.11).

The principal selected explanatory notes that should be provided (if the information is material and not provided elsewhere in the report) are as follows (IAS 34.16A):
(i)   a statement that the same accounting policies and methods of computation are used in the interim financial statements, as compared

with the most recent annual financial statements, or a description of the nature and effect of any changes

(ii)   explanatory comments about the seasonality or cyclicality of interim operations

(iii) the nature and amount of changes to estimates reported in prior financial years

(iv) issues, repurchases and repayments of debt and equity

(v)   dividends paid

(vi) certain segment information, if required by IFRS 8

(vii) material events subsequent to the end of the interim period that have not been reflected in the financial statements for the interim period

(viii) the effect of changes in the composition of the Group during the interim period (e.g. business combinations)

(ix) changes in contingent liabilities or contingent assets since the end of the last reporting period.

Appendix I – Workings

Basic EPS 2x10 and 2x09

(1) Earnings (the numerator)

Earnings for the purposes of computing EPS is defined as profit attributable to ordinary shareholders of the parent entity (IAS 33.10).

In the case of the Campbell Group, earnings will therefore be computed as follows:

	2x10 €'m	2x09 €'m
Profit for the year attributable to owners of the parent	1,200	870
Less preference dividend		
– on 10% Irredeemable Pref. Shares	(20)	(20)
Earnings	1,180	850

(2) Weighted average number of shares for Basic EPS (the denominator)

Date	Particulars	Movement	Cum. Shares (M)	*No. x Time Prop. x Bonus Factor x Rights Multiplier*	Weighted Ave. No. (M)
1.1.'10	B'Fwd (W3)	-	800 ✓	[800m x 1/12 x 2/1 x €2.50/€2.40]	138.9
1.2.'10	Rights issue	200 ✓	1,000 ✓	[1,000m x 2/12 x 2/1]	333.3
1.4.'10	Issue at fair value	200 ✓	1,200 ✓	[1,200m x 3/12 x 2/1]	600
1.7.'10	Bonus issue	1,200 ✓	2,400 ✓	[2,400m x 3/12]	600
1.10.'10	Treasury purchase	(100) ✓	2,300 ✓	[2,300m x 3/12]	575
	Weighted average number of shares for Basic EPS				2,247.2

share buy back

(3) Theoretical ex-rights price (TERP)

			€
Cum rights	4	@ €2.50	10.00
Rights	1	@ €2.00	2.00
Ex Rights	5		12.00

Theoretical ex-rights price = €12.00/5 = €2.40 per share.

Therefore, the rights multiplier is €2.50/€2.40.

(4) Diluted earnings per share for 2x10

Entities are required to calculate diluted earnings per share attributable to ordinary equity shareholders of the parent company (IAS 33.30).

For the purpose of calculating diluted EPS, an entity shall adjust profit or loss, and the weighted average number of shares outstanding for the effects of all dilutive potential ordinary shares (IAS 33.31).

For the Campbell Group, there are two sources of dilutive potential ordinary shares:

- Share options issued on the 1 April 2x10
- €500 million of 8% convertible debentures.

The computation of diluted EPS may require adjustments to be made to both earnings and the number of shares:

Earnings

In the case of the 8% **convertible debentures**, the profit attributable to ordinary equity holders of the parent entity should be adjusted by the after-tax effect of interest recognised in the period (IAS 33.33). For the Campbell Group, profit will be increased by €28 million (i.e. €500m x 8% x .7).

In respect of the **share options**, there is no effect on earnings.

Shares

For the purpose of calculating diluted EPS, the number of ordinary shares is the weighted average number of issued ordinary shares, plus the weighted average number of ordinary shares that *would* be issued on the conversion of all the dilutive potential ordinary shares into ordinary shares (IAS 33.36). Dilutive potential ordinary shares should be deemed to have been converted into ordinary shares at the beginning of the period, or the date of issue if later (IAS 33.36).

For the **8% convertible debentures**, the additional number of ordinary shares is 250m (i.e. €500m/100 x 50).

For **share options**, potential ordinary shares are treated as consisting of both of the following (IAS 33.46):

(i) **A contract to issue ordinary shares at their average market price during the period.** Such ordinary shares are assumed to be fairly priced and to be neither dilutive nor anti-dilutive. For the Campbell Group this will be computed as follows:

- Average market price of one ordinary share during 2x10 = €2.50
- Weighted average number of shares under option during 2x10 = 150m (i.e.10 x 20m x 9/12)

- Exercise price for shares under option during 2x10 = €2
- Weighted average number of shares that would have been issued at average market price = 120m (i.e. 150m x €2/€2.5)

(ii) **A contract to issue the remaining ordinary shares for no consideration.** Such ordinary shares generate no proceeds and have no effect on profit or loss attributable to ordinary shares outstanding. Therefore, such shares are dilutive and are added to the number of ordinary shares outstanding in the calculation of diluted EPS.

For the Campbell Group, the number of shares deemed to be issued for no consideration will be 30m (i.e. 150m – 120m).

Calculation of Diluted EPS

In considering whether potential ordinary shares are dilutive or anti-dilutive, each issue is considered separately, in sequence, from the most dilutive to the least dilutive. Thus, dilutive potential ordinary shares with the lowest 'earnings per incremental share' are included in the diluted EPS calculation before those that have a higher earnings per incremental share (IAS 33.44). This is to avoid an anti-dilutive issue being allowed to impact on the diluted EPS figure.

This requirement of IAS 33 is applied as follows:

	Increase in earnings	Increase in number of ordinary shares	Earnings per incremental share
Share options	Nil	Shares for no consideration = 30m	Nil
8% Convertible debentures	€28m	250m	11.2 cent

Potential ordinary shares should be treated as dilutive only when their conversion to ordinary shares would decrease EPS from continuing operations (IAS 33.41). Potential ordinary shares are only included in the computation of diluted EPS when their effect on EPS is dilutive (IAS 33.43).

WELCOME TO MEETINGS NOT STARTING WITHOUT YOU

Chartered Accountants work at the highest levels in Irish business. In fact six out of ten Irish Chartered Accountants work at Finance Director level or above.

Discover our flexible training options:

CharteredCareers.ie

Chartered Accountants Ireland